AF680081

CONTENTS

ABOUT THIS BOOK

Why ESG Matters for finance professionals

"In today's interconnected world, integrating Environmental, Social, and Governance principles is no longer optional for finance professionals. ESG is reshaping investment strategies, financial reporting, and risk management."

Who Is This Book For?

"This book is for finance professionals, including CFOs, auditors, analysts, and financial managers, who want to better understand ESG principles and apply them effectively in their roles."

Key Benefits:

- Practical knowledge of ESG frameworks
- Insights into financial reporting with ESG metrics
- Case studies and actionable strategies for implementation

I am a seasoned finance professional with a passion for integrating Environmental, Social, and Governance (ESG) principles into corporate finance and reporting. This book is based on ongoing research I am conducting in the field of ESG, where I closely follow the topic, document its evolution, and analyze emerging trends impacting finance professionals.

With a solid foundation as an Associate Chartered Management Accountant (ACMA) with a Master's degree in Finance and Accounting, I bring a unique blend of technical expertise and forward-thinking insights to help finance leaders navigate the ever-changing ESG landscape.

As the ESG field continues to grow and reshape financial practices globally, this book serves as both a practical guide and a reflection of real-time developments, ensuring readers stay ahead of the curve in this critical area.

Sekai FM

© 2024 Sekai FM | ESG for finance professionals

ABOUT THIS BOOK

© 2024, Sekai FM
All rights reserved.
No part of this publication may be reproduced, distributed, or transmitted in any form or by any means, including photocopying, recording, or other electronic or mechanical methods, without the prior written permission of the publisher, except in the case of brief quotations embodied in critical reviews and certain other non-commercial uses permitted by copyright law.

Published by Sekai F Matanhire
ISBN: 9798230379973

1

Introduction

1. ESG for finance professionals - An Introduction
2. The Role of finance professionals in ESG Reporting
3. ESG and the Evolving Role of Finance Reporting

Section 1: ESG for finance professionals - An Introduction

Understanding ESG: Why It Matters for Finance

In recent years, the business landscape has been reshaped by an increasing emphasis on sustainability, ethical practices, and long-term value creation. Environmental, Social, and Governance (ESG) considerations have emerged as critical pillars in this transformation, influencing the decisions of investors, regulators, and corporate stakeholders alike.

For finance professionals, ESG is no longer a peripheral concern but a central factor in assessing risk, shaping strategy, and ensuring the resilience of financial performance.

ESG is not merely a set of abstract principles - it is a measurable, actionable framework that ties corporate performance to sustainable outcomes. Each of its components reflects distinct yet interconnected priorities:

- **Environmental (E)**: Assessing how a company impacts and depends on natural ecosystems, including carbon emissions, energy use, waste management, and biodiversity.
- **Social (S)**: Evaluating a company's influence on people, from employee welfare and diversity to community engagement and human rights practices.
- **Governance (G)**: Examining the structures, policies, and ethical standards guiding leadership, risk management, and transparency.

Finance professionals play a pivotal role in ESG integration because they possess the expertise to translate these qualitative factors into quantifiable metrics that can inform decision-making. Whether calculating the financial risks of climate change, evaluating the return on social initiatives, or ensuring ethical governance practices, their skills are indispensable to creating value in an ESG-conscious world.

The Shift from Traditional Finance to ESG Integration

Historically, financial analysis focused predominantly on profitability, solvency, and market performance. While these metrics remain critical, the limitations of a purely financial lens have become increasingly evident. The 2008 global financial crisis and subsequent environmental and social challenges underscored the systemic risks posed by governance failures, unsustainable practices, and social inequality. This led to a paradigm shift: stakeholders began to demand a more holistic understanding of corporate value that accounts for non-financial performance and long-term sustainability.

Investors, in particular, are driving the integration of ESG into financial decision-making. ESG factors are no longer optional considerations but are increasingly seen as essential indicators of a company's risk profile, resilience, and competitive positioning.

Section 1: ESG for finance professionals - An Introduction

The Shift from Traditional Finance to ESG Integration
For finance professionals, this shift requires new skills and perspectives. Traditional financial analysis must now intersect with ESG metrics to evaluate risks such as:

Reputational Risk
The potential damage to a company's brand and market value due to poor ESG performance.

Operational Risk
Disruptions stemming from resource scarcity, labour issues, or supply chain vulnerabilities.

Climate Risk
The financial impact of climate change on assets, supply chains, and operations

Compliance Risk
The costs of non-compliance with emerging ESG regulations.

Why ESG Matters to finance professionals
The incorporation of ESG into financial reporting is more than a regulatory obligation - it is a strategic imperative. Research consistently shows that companies with strong ESG performance tend to outperform their peers in the long term.

A 2022 study by MSCI found that companies with high ESG ratings experienced lower cost of capital, greater operational efficiency, and higher shareholder returns. These outcomes align with the objectives of finance professionals: to safeguard assets, optimize performance, and create sustainable value for stakeholders.

For CFOs, controllers, and other finance professionals, ESG reporting represents an opportunity to enhance transparency, improve investor confidence, and align corporate strategy with global sustainability goals. Yet, this opportunity also comes with challenges. ESG data is often fragmented, inconsistent, and difficult to measure. Moreover, the rapidly evolving regulatory landscape requires finance professionals to stay informed and agile.

In this book, we aim to demystify ESG reporting for finance professionals, providing actionable insights, tools, and frameworks to navigate this complex but rewarding field. By mastering ESG principles, finance professionals can not only meet regulatory expectations but also position themselves as leaders in driving corporate transformation and sustainable growth.

Section 2: The Role of finance professionals in ESG Reporting

The integration of Environmental, Social, and Governance (ESG) factors into business operations has expanded the traditional responsibilities of finance professionals. No longer confined to managing balance sheets and financial statements, they are now at the forefront of translating non-financial performance into measurable, actionable insights. This shift is transforming how businesses operate, evaluate risk, and communicate value, positioning finance professionals as key drivers in the ESG ecosystem.

1. Bridging ESG and Financial Performance

At its core, ESG reporting seeks to connect a company's sustainable practices with its financial outcomes. finance professionals play a crucial role in achieving this alignment by leveraging their expertise in data analysis, financial modeling, and risk assessment. Their ability to quantify the financial implications of ESG initiatives enables stakeholders to understand how sustainability strategies impact profitability, cost structure, and long-term value creation. For example:

Environmental Metrics

Finance professionals can assess the monetary implications of carbon reduction initiatives, such as cost savings from energy efficiency or the financial risks of regulatory penalties for exceeding emission limits.

Social Metrics

They quantify the impact of employee retention programs, diversity initiatives, and community engagement efforts on operational efficiency and brand reputation.

Governance Metrics

By analyzing board diversity, executive compensation, and governance frameworks, finance professionals provide critical insights into how ethical leadership contributes to shareholder value.

This capacity to link ESG metrics with financial performance is indispensable for decision-making at the board and investor levels. It transforms ESG from an abstract concept into a measurable component of business strategy, aligning it with financial objectives and stakeholder expectations.

2. Navigating ESG Data Challenges

One of the most significant challenges in ESG reporting is the lack of standardized data and the complexity of measuring qualitative factors. Unlike traditional financial metrics, which follow established accounting standards, ESG data often comes from diverse and inconsistent sources, such as sustainability reports, supplier disclosures, and third-party assessments. This lack of uniformity can lead to inaccuracies and hinder comparability across industries and geographies.

Section 2: The Role of finance professionals in ESG Reporting

2. Navigating ESG Data Challenges
Finance professionals are uniquely equipped to address these challenges by applying robust data governance practices to ESG reporting. Their expertise in:

- Data Collection and Validation: Ensures the accuracy and reliability of ESG inputs, whether they come from internal systems, external stakeholders, or emerging technologies like IoT and blockchain.

- Materiality Assessment: Helps prioritize the ESG factors most relevant to a company's financial performance and stakeholder interests, ensuring the efficient allocation of resources.

- Integration of Financial and Non-Financial Data: Bridges the gap between ESG metrics and traditional accounting systems, creating a unified reporting framework that enhances transparency and decision-making.

By refining how ESG data is collected, analyzed, and presented, finance professionals enable organizations to produce credible reports that satisfy regulatory requirements and inspire investor confidence.

3. Managing ESG-Related Risks
As ESG considerations become integral to business strategy, finance professionals are tasked with identifying and mitigating a range of ESG-related risks. These risks often intersect with traditional financial concerns but require a deeper understanding of sustainability dynamics. Key areas of focus include:

- Climate Risk: Finance professionals assess the potential impact of climate change on asset valuation, insurance premiums, and operational costs. This includes analyzing risks such as extreme weather events, resource scarcity, and transitioning to low-carbon operations.

- Regulatory Risk: As governments worldwide tighten ESG-related regulations, companies face higher compliance costs and potential penalties for non-compliance. finance professionals ensure that reporting frameworks are aligned with evolving standards, mitigating exposure to regulatory scrutiny.

- Reputational Risk: ESG performance directly affects brand equity and stakeholder trust. finance professionals quantify the financial implications of reputational damage stemming from poor ESG practices, such as supply chain labour violations or environmental disasters.

Proactively managing these risks not only protects a company's bottom line but also enhances its long-term resilience and competitiveness.

Section 2: The Role of finance professionals in ESG Reporting

4. Supporting Strategic Decision-Making and Capital Allocation

ESG reporting is not merely a compliance exercise - it is a strategic tool for identifying opportunities, driving innovation, and allocating resources effectively. finance professionals play a critical role in embedding ESG into decision-making processes by providing data-driven insights and aligning sustainability initiatives with financial goals. Examples of strategic contributions include:

By incorporating ESG into strategic decision-making, finance professionals enhance the organization's ability to adapt to evolving market conditions and stakeholder expectations.

Data Collection & Validation
Ensures the accuracy and reliability of ESG inputs, whether they come from internal systems, external stakeholders, or emerging technologies like IoT and blockchain.

Materiality Assessment
Helps prioritize the ESG factors most relevant to a company's financial performance and stakeholder interests, ensuring the efficient allocation of resources.

Integration of Financial & Non-Financial Data
Bridges the gap between ESG metrics and traditional accounting systems, creating a unified reporting framework that enhances transparency and decision-making.

5. Driving Stakeholder Communication and Transparency

The demand for transparent and meaningful ESG disclosures has grown exponentially, driven by investors, regulators, and consumers. finance professionals are essential in crafting these disclosures, ensuring they are both accurate and compelling.Their contributions include:

- Aligning ESG Reporting with Stakeholder Needs: Finance professionals identify the metrics that matter most to investors, regulators, and customers, tailoring disclosures to address these priorities.

- Building Trust Through Assurance: Collaborating with internal auditors and external assurance providers to validate ESG data, enhancing credibility and reducing greenwashing risks.

- Integrating ESG into Financial Communications: Embedding ESG narratives into investor presentations, annual reports, and other communications, demonstrating how sustainability drives value.

Effective communication not only fulfills regulatory requirements but also strengthens relationships with stakeholders, positioning the organization as a leader in transparency and accountability.

Section 2: The Role of finance professionals in ESG Reporting

6. The Transformational Role of finance professionals

The role of finance professionals in ESG reporting is transformative, redefining the boundaries of finance and sustainability. By applying their analytical expertise to ESG challenges, they are not only meeting the demands of the present but also shaping the future of corporate accountability. Their work ensures that ESG is not just a reporting obligation but a strategic advantage, enabling businesses to create long-term value for all stakeholders.

Section 3: ESG and the Evolving Role of Financial Reporting

The incorporation of Environmental, Social, and Governance (ESG) factors into corporate strategy has expanded the scope of financial reporting beyond traditional measures of profitability and solvency. ESG reporting reflects the growing recognition that financial performance cannot be fully understood without considering the environmental, social, and governance risks and opportunities that organizations face. For finance professionals, this shift represents both a challenge and an opportunity to redefine the purpose and impact of financial reporting in the 21st century.

1. From Shareholder Value to Stakeholder Value

Historically, the purpose of financial reporting was to provide accurate and timely information to shareholders, with the primary goal of maximizing returns. This approach often prioritized short-term financial performance over long-term sustainability. However, the emergence of ESG principles has broadened the focus of financial reporting to encompass the needs of a wider range of stakeholders, including employees, customers, regulators, and communities.

This shift from shareholder value to stakeholder value has profound implications for finance professionals:

- Holistic Value Creation: ESG reporting demonstrates how an organization's non-financial performance contributes to long-term value creation. For example, a company's investment in renewable energy may reduce operational costs while enhancing its reputation with environmentally conscious consumers and investors.

- Transparent Accountability: ESG reporting holds organizations accountable for their impact on the environment and society, ensuring that finance professionals provide accurate disclosures that reflect the true costs and benefits of corporate activities.

- Strategic Alignment: By integrating ESG factors into financial reports, organizations can better align their business strategies with stakeholder expectations, fostering trust and long-term loyalty.

For finance professionals, adapting to this paradigm shift requires a deeper understanding of how ESG metrics complement traditional financial measures and how these metrics can be communicated effectively to diverse stakeholders.

Section 3: ESG and the Evolving Role of Financial Reporting

2. The Integration of ESG and Financial Reporting

Integrating ESG metrics into financial reporting is a complex but necessary step toward providing a complete picture of an organization's performance and prospects. This integration involves linking ESG initiatives to financial outcomes, enabling stakeholders to assess the materiality of sustainability efforts on a company's bottom line. Key aspects of ESG-financial integration include:

- **Linking ESG to Financial Statements**: We are tasked with embedding ESG considerations into key financial documents, such as annual reports and management discussion and analysis sections, e.g. climate-related risks can be reflected in asset impairment assessments or provisions for future liabilities.

- **Cost-Benefit Analysis:** Organizations need to quantify the financial implications of ESG initiatives, such as the return on investment (ROI) of energy-efficient equipment or the cost savings from reducing waste.

- **Materiality Assessment:** Finance professionals must identify the ESG factors that are most relevant to their organization's financial performance. For example, water usage may be a material issue for a beverage company but less significant for a software firm.

3. ESG Reporting Standards and Their Impact on Financial Reporting

The proliferation of ESG reporting frameworks, such as the Global Reporting Initiative (GRI), the Sustainability Accounting Standards Board (SASB), and the Task Force on Climate-related Financial Disclosures (TCFD), has added complexity to the reporting landscape. For finance professionals, navigating these standards is essential to ensuring that ESG disclosures are consistent, comparable, and aligned with regulatory requirements.

Section 3: ESG and the Evolving Role of Financial Reporting

3. ESG Reporting Standards and Their Impact on Financial Reporting
Some of the critical impacts of these standards on financial reporting include:

- Standardized Disclosures: Frameworks like SASB emphasize the materiality of ESG factors in financial reporting, providing industry-specific guidelines that help organizations prioritize relevant disclosures.

- Climate-Related Risk Reporting: The TCFD framework has made climate-related financial disclosures a priority for regulators and investors, requiring organizations to assess and report the financial implications of physical and transition risks.

- Emerging Double Materiality Perspective: This concept, increasingly adopted in regions like the European Union, requires companies to consider not only how ESG factors impact their financial performance but also how their operations impact the environment and society.

Adapting to these standards requires finance professionals to stay informed about regulatory developments, invest in training, and collaborate with sustainability teams to ensure comprehensive and accurate reporting.

4. Challenges in ESG Reporting for finance professionals
Despite its growing importance, ESG reporting presents several challenges for finance professionals, including data quality, comparability, and the integration of non-financial metrics into traditional financial frameworks. Key challenges include:

- Data Fragmentation: ESG data often comes from disparate sources, making it difficult to ensure consistency and reliability. For instance, emissions data may be collected from operations, suppliers, or third-party audits, each with varying degrees of accuracy.

- Lack of Standardization: While progress has been made, the lack of globally unified ESG reporting standards creates inconsistencies that complicate cross-company and cross-industry comparisons.

- Evolving Regulatory Landscape: The rapid pace of regulatory changes in ESG reporting requires finance professionals to stay agile and adapt quickly to new disclosure requirements.

To address these challenges, we must adopt robust data management practices, leverage technology for real-time data collection and analysis, and collaborate with cross-functional teams to ensure alignment between ESG and financial reporting processes.

© 2024 Sekai FM | ESG for finance professionals

Section 3: ESG and the Evolving Role of Financial Reporting

5. Opportunities for finance professionals

While ESG reporting presents challenges, it also offers significant opportunities for finance professionals to enhance their roles and add strategic value:

- Leadership in Sustainability: By mastering ESG reporting, finance professionals can position themselves as leaders in driving their organization's sustainability agenda, influencing decision-making at the highest levels.

- Enhanced Skill Sets: The integration of ESG into financial reporting requires new competencies, such as climate risk modeling, supply chain analysis, and stakeholder communication, which can enhance career prospects and professional growth.

- Creating Competitive Advantage: Organizations with robust ESG reporting practices are better positioned to attract investors, reduce capital costs, and build resilient business models. finance professionals are critical to achieving these outcomes by ensuring that ESG efforts are strategically aligned and financially sound.

Conclusion

ESG as a Transformational Force in Financial Reporting. The evolving role of ESG in financial reporting represents a fundamental transformation in how organizations measure and communicate value. For finance professionals, this shift is both a challenge and an opportunity-requiring new skills, tools, and perspectives but offering a chance to lead in an era of sustainable finance. By embracing ESG reporting, finance professionals not only enhance their organization's transparency and accountability but also contribute to a more sustainable and equitable global economy.

2

ESG Reporting and the Regulatory Landscape

1. Key ESG Regulations and Standards
2. Global Trends & Regional Differences in ESG Regulation
3. Compliance and Legal Considerations for ESG Reporting

© 2024 Sekai FM | ESG for finance professionals

Section 1: Key ESG Regulations and Standards for finance professionals

The regulatory landscape for Environmental, Social, and Governance (ESG) reporting has evolved rapidly over the past decade, reflecting heightened awareness of sustainability issues and the growing demand for corporate accountability. For finance professionals, understanding and navigating these regulations is critical, as ESG compliance increasingly intersects with financial reporting obligations. This section provides an overview of the key global ESG regulations and standards shaping the field, highlighting their implications for finance professionals.

1. The Evolution of ESG Regulation

The emergence of ESG regulation is rooted in the recognition that financial markets play a pivotal role in addressing global challenges such as climate change, social inequality, and corporate governance failures. Policymakers and regulatory bodies around the world have introduced frameworks and standards designed to promote transparency, accountability, and sustainability in corporate practices.

Key milestones in ESG regulation include:

The Paris Agreement	**The Task Force on Climate-related Financial Disclosures**	**EU Non-Financial Reporting Directive**
This global climate accord set the stage for climate-focused regulations, encouraging countries to reduce greenhouse gas emissions and mobilize climate finance.	*Established voluntary guidelines for climate risk reporting, which have become a global benchmark for climate-related financial disclosures.*	*Among the first regulations mandating non-financial disclosures, requiring large companies to report on environmental, social, and governance factors.*
2015	**2014**	**2017**

These initiatives laid the groundwork for a regulatory environment where ESG reporting is no longer optional but a critical aspect of corporate governance and financial strategy.

Section 1: Key ESG Regulations and Standards for finance professionals

2. Key Global ESG Reporting Standards

A range of ESG reporting standards has emerged to guide organizations in their disclosure efforts. While many of these standards are voluntary, they are increasingly adopted by companies and supported by regulators as part of their compliance frameworks. finance professionals must be familiar with these standards to ensure accurate, relevant, and comparable ESG disclosures.

- Global Reporting Initiative (GRI):
  - Overview: One of the most widely used ESG reporting frameworks, GRI provides a comprehensive set of standards for disclosing an organization's economic, environmental, and social impacts.
  - Relevance for finance professionals: GRI emphasizes transparency and stakeholder engagement, helping finance professionals identify and report material ESG risks and opportunities.

- Sustainability Accounting Standards Board (SASB):
  - Overview: SASB focuses on industry-specific standards, linking ESG factors to financial performance.
  - Relevance for finance professionals: SASB's emphasis on financial materiality aligns ESG disclosures with traditional financial reporting, making it highly relevant for investors and analysts.

- Task Force on Climate-related Financial Disclosures (TCFD):
  - Overview: TCFD provides a framework for climate-related risk disclosure, emphasizing governance, strategy, risk management, and metrics.
  - Relevance for finance professionals: TCFD's focus on integrating climate risks into financial statements is essential for organizations managing climate-related financial exposures.

- Corporate Sustainability Reporting Directive (CSRD):
  - Overview: Introduced by the European Union, the CSRD expands on the NFRD by requiring detailed ESG disclosures and aligning with international standards such as GRI and TCFD.
  - Relevance for finance professionals: The CSRD places a strong emphasis on double materiality, requiring companies to report both their impact on sustainability and how sustainability affects their financial performance.

- International Sustainability Standards Board (ISSB):
  - Overview: Established by the IFRS Foundation, the ISSB aims to create a unified global standard for ESG reporting, integrating key elements of SASB and TCFD.
  - Relevance for finance professionals: As a global initiative, ISSB standards are expected to harmonize ESG reporting, simplifying compliance and improving comparability.

Section 1: Key ESG Regulations and Standards for finance professionals

2. Key Global ESG Reporting Standards

A range of ESG reporting standards has emerged to guide organizations in their disclosure efforts. While many of these standards are voluntary, they are increasingly adopted by companies and supported by regulators as part of their compliance frameworks. finance professionals must be familiar with these standards to ensure accurate, relevant, and comparable ESG disclosures.

- Global Reporting Initiative (GRI):
  - Overview: One of the most widely used ESG reporting frameworks, GRI provides a comprehensive set of standards for disclosing an organization's economic, environmental, and social impacts.
  - Relevance for finance professionals: GRI emphasizes transparency and stakeholder engagement, helping finance professionals identify and report material ESG risks and opportunities.

- Sustainability Accounting Standards Board (SASB):
  - Overview: SASB focuses on industry-specific standards, linking ESG factors to financial performance.
  - Relevance for finance professionals: SASB's emphasis on financial materiality aligns ESG disclosures with traditional financial reporting, making it highly relevant for investors and analysts.

- Task Force on Climate-related Financial Disclosures (TCFD):
  - Overview: TCFD provides a framework for climate-related risk disclosure, emphasizing governance, strategy, risk management, and metrics.
  - Relevance for finance professionals: TCFD's focus on integrating climate risks into financial statements is essential for organizations managing climate-related financial exposures.

- Corporate Sustainability Reporting Directive (CSRD):
  - Overview: Introduced by the European Union, the CSRD expands on the NFRD by requiring detailed ESG disclosures and aligning with international standards such as GRI and TCFD.
  - Relevance for finance professionals: The CSRD places a strong emphasis on double materiality, requiring companies to report both their impact on sustainability and how sustainability affects their financial performance.

- International Sustainability Standards Board (ISSB):
  - Overview: Established by the IFRS Foundation, the ISSB aims to create a unified global standard for ESG reporting, integrating key elements of SASB and TCFD.
  - Relevance for finance professionals: As a global initiative, ISSB standards are expected to harmonize ESG reporting, simplifying compliance and improving comparability.

Section 1: Key ESG Regulations and Standards for finance professionals

3. Regional Variations in ESG Regulation

While global standards provide a foundation, ESG regulations vary significantly by region, reflecting differences in policy priorities, market maturity, and stakeholder expectations. Financial professionals must be aware of these regional nuances to ensure compliance and address stakeholder demands effectively.

- Europe:
  - The European Union leads the world in ESG regulation, with initiatives such as the CSRD, the EU Taxonomy for Sustainable Activities, and the Sustainable Finance Disclosure Regulation (SFDR). These frameworks promote transparency and aim to redirect capital flows toward sustainable investments.
  - Implications for Financial Professionals: European companies must adopt rigorous ESG reporting practices, often incorporating double materiality and detailed climate-related disclosures.

- United States:
  - ESG regulation in the U.S. is more fragmented but gaining momentum. The Securities and Exchange Commission (SEC) has proposed rules requiring public companies to disclose climate-related risks and greenhouse gas emissions.
  - Implications for Financial Professionals: U.S. companies are increasingly expected to align with global standards like TCFD while navigating state-level variations in ESG requirements.

- Asia-Pacific:
  - ESG regulation in the Asia-Pacific region varies widely, with countries like Japan and Singapore adopting progressive frameworks, while others are still in the early stages of ESG integration.
  - Implications for Financial Professionals: Multinational companies operating in the region must adapt to a patchwork of regulations, balancing global standards with local expectations.

- Emerging Markets:
  - In emerging markets, ESG regulation is often driven by international investors and development finance institutions. Frameworks like the IFC's Performance Standards provide guidance for companies operating in these regions.
  - Implications for Financial Professionals: ESG reporting in emerging markets often focuses on social and governance factors, reflecting regional priorities such as labor rights and anti-corruption measures.

Section 1: Key ESG Regulations and Standards for finance professionals

4. The Role of finance professionals in ESG Compliance

Finance professionals are central to ensuring that organizations comply with ESG regulations and standards. Their responsibilities include:

- Monitoring Regulatory Developments: Staying informed about changes in ESG regulations and proactively adapting reporting practices to meet new requirements.
- Aligning ESG and Financial Reporting: Integrating ESG disclosures into financial statements and annual reports, ensuring consistency with global standards.
- Supporting Assurance and Verification: Collaborating with auditors to validate ESG data, enhancing credibility and stakeholder trust.
- Engaging with Regulators: Providing accurate and timely information to regulators, addressing inquiries, and ensuring compliance with disclosure mandates.

By fulfilling these responsibilities, finance professionals help organizations navigate the complex regulatory landscape and maintain their license to operate in increasingly ESG-focused markets.

Conclusion

The regulatory landscape for ESG reporting is complex and dynamic, reflecting the growing importance of sustainability in global markets. finance professionals play a critical role in ensuring compliance with these regulations, integrating ESG into financial reporting, and aligning corporate practices with stakeholder expectations. Mastery of key ESG standards and frameworks is essential for navigating this landscape and positioning organizations for long-term success. The next section will delve into global trends in ESG regulation and explore how finance professionals can stay ahead of emerging requirements.

Section 2: Global Trends and Regional Differences in ESG Regulation

As sustainability becomes a critical component of global business strategy, the regulatory landscape for Environmental, Social, and Governance (ESG) reporting is evolving at an unprecedented pace. finance professionals must understand the global trends shaping ESG regulation and how regional differences influence compliance and reporting practices. This section explores these dynamics, highlighting key developments and their implications for financial reporting.

1. Global Trends Driving ESG Regulation

Several overarching trends are shaping ESG regulation across the world, reflecting the growing demand for transparency, accountability, and sustainability in corporate practices. These trends provide insight into the direction of future regulatory developments and the role finance professionals play in adapting to them.

1.1. Shift from Voluntary to Mandatory Reporting

- *While ESG reporting has traditionally been voluntary, a growing number of jurisdictions are introducing mandatory disclosure requirements. This shift reflects the increasing recognition of ESG factors as material to financial performance and systemic stability.*
    - ***Examples:***
        - *The European Union's Corporate Sustainability Reporting Directive (CSRD) mandates ESG disclosures for thousands of companies, expanding the scope of the earlier Non-Financial Reporting Directive (NFRD).*
        - *The U.S. Securities and Exchange Commission (SEC) is moving toward mandatory climate-related disclosures for publicly traded companies.*

1.2. Harmonization of ESG Standards

- *The proliferation of ESG frameworks has created challenges for comparability and consistency. In response, global efforts are underway to harmonize ESG standards, making it easier for organizations to align with regulatory and investor expectations.*
- *The International Sustainability Standards Board (ISSB), established by the IFRS Foundation, is working to consolidate frameworks like SASB and TCFD into a unified global standard.*

1.3. Integration of Climate Risk into Financial Reporting

- *Climate risk is at the forefront of ESG regulation, with an emphasis on integrating climate-related disclosures into financial reporting. Regulators and investors increasingly expect organizations to assess and disclose the financial implications of physical and transition risks associated with climate change.*

1.4. Focus on Double Materiality

- *Many regulators, particularly in the European Union, are adopting the principle of double materiality, which requires companies to disclose both:*
    - *How sustainability factors affect their financial performance.*
    - *Their impact on the environment and society.*

1.5. Increasing Scrutiny of Social and Governance Factors

- *While environmental factors dominate the ESG conversation, there is growing regulatory focus on social and governance issues. Topics such as human rights, labor practices, diversity, and board accountability are gaining prominence in ESG reporting requirements.*

Section 3: Compliance and Legal Considerations for ESG Reporting

The integration of Environmental, Social, and Governance (ESG) factors into regulatory frameworks has not only expanded the scope of reporting requirements but also heightened the compliance and legal risks associated with non-financial disclosures. finance professionals must navigate this complex landscape with precision, ensuring that ESG reports meet legal standards while safeguarding the organization against potential liabilities. This section explores the critical compliance and legal considerations in ESG reporting, emphasizing their implications for finance professionals.

1. The Legal Foundations of ESG Reporting

The legal underpinnings of ESG reporting arise from a combination of national regulations, international standards, and voluntary frameworks that have been codified into mandatory requirements in many jurisdictions. While the specific legal obligations vary by region, they generally fall into three broad categories:

- Mandatory Disclosure Requirements:
  - Many jurisdictions now require companies to report on ESG-related risks and opportunities as part of their annual financial disclosures. Examples include the EU's Corporate Sustainability Reporting Directive (CSRD) and the SEC's proposed climate disclosure rules.
  - Legal foundations for these mandates often stem from broader corporate governance laws and securities regulations, which aim to ensure transparency and protect investors.

- Materiality-Based Reporting Obligations:
  - Regulations such as the Task Force on Climate-related Financial Disclosures (TCFD) emphasize the need to report ESG factors that materially impact a company's financial performance or pose risks to stakeholders.
  - Finance professionals are responsible for identifying and prioritizing material ESG issues, ensuring their accurate representation in financial statements.

- Voluntary Frameworks with Legal Implications:
  - Even voluntary ESG standards, such as the Global Reporting Initiative (GRI) or Sustainability Accounting Standards Board (SASB), can carry legal weight if companies choose to adopt them. Failing to adhere to these standards once declared can lead to accusations of misrepresentation or greenwashing.

Understanding the legal foundations of ESG reporting helps finance professionals align disclosures with regulatory expectations while minimizing exposure to litigation and regulatory penalties.

Section 3: Compliance and Legal Considerations for ESG Reporting

2. Key Compliance Challenges in ESG Reporting

Compliance with ESG reporting regulations is complex, particularly given the dynamic and fragmented nature of the global regulatory environment. finance professionals must address several key challenges to ensure adherence to legal standards:

2.1. Data Accuracy and Completeness

- Challenge: ESG data often originates from multiple sources, including supply chains, internal systems, and third-party providers. Ensuring the accuracy, completeness, and reliability of this data is critical for compliance.
- Implication: Inaccurate or incomplete data can result in misleading disclosures, exposing organizations to regulatory scrutiny and legal liability.

2.2. Evolving Regulations

- Challenge: The regulatory landscape for ESG reporting is evolving rapidly, with frequent updates to disclosure requirements, thresholds, and methodologies.
- Implication: Finance professionals must stay informed about emerging regulations and ensure that reporting processes remain adaptable and up-to-date.

2.3. Cross-Jurisdictional Compliance

- Challenge: Multinational organizations face the added complexity of complying with ESG regulations across multiple jurisdictions, each with its own requirements and enforcement mechanisms.
- Implication: Divergent standards may lead to inconsistencies in reporting, increasing the risk of non-compliance and reputational damage.

2.4. Legal Risks of Greenwashing

- Challenge: Companies that exaggerate or falsify their ESG performance may be accused of greenwashing, leading to lawsuits, regulatory penalties, and reputational harm.
- Implication: Finance professionals play a crucial role in ensuring that ESG disclosures are accurate, evidence-based, and free from misleading claims.

Section 3: Compliance and Legal Considerations for ESG Reporting

3. Legal Risks and Liabilities in ESG Reporting

The legal risks associated with ESG reporting are significant, particularly as regulators, investors, and other stakeholders scrutinize disclosures more closely. Finance professionals must be aware of these risks and take proactive steps to mitigate them.

Misrepresentation & Fraud	**Risk**: Inaccurate or incomplete ESG disclosures can be deemed misleading, resulting in claims of fraud or misrepresentation. **Mitigation**: Implement robust data validation processes and align ESG disclosures with established reporting frameworks to ensure accuracy and transparency.
Non-Compliance	**Risk**: Failure to comply with mandatory ESG disclosure requirements can result in fines, sanctions, and loss of investor confidence. **Mitigation**: Regularly monitor regulatory updates and engage with legal and compliance teams to ensure adherence to reporting obligations.
Stakeholder Litigation	**Risk**: Investors, consumers, and advocacy groups may sue companies for failing to meet stated ESG commitments or for causing harm to the environment or society. **Mitigation**: Maintain comprehensive documentation of ESG initiatives, ensure third-party audits of ESG data, and address stakeholder concerns proactively.

Section 3: Compliance and Legal Considerations for ESG Reporting

4. Best Practices for ESG Compliance

To navigate the compliance and legal challenges of ESG reporting, finance professionals should adopt the following best practices:

4.1. Establish Robust Governance Structures

- Create cross-functional ESG committees that include finance, legal, compliance, and sustainability teams.
- Develop clear accountability frameworks to ensure that ESG responsibilities are well-defined and properly executed.

4.2. Invest in Technology and Automation

- Leverage ESG reporting tools and data analytics platforms to streamline data collection, validation, and reporting.
- Use automation to reduce errors and enhance the accuracy of ESG disclosures.

4.3. Conduct Regular Materiality Assessments

- Periodically review and update materiality assessments to ensure that ESG disclosures reflect the most relevant risks and opportunities.
- Engage stakeholders in the materiality assessment process to align reporting with their expectations.

4.4. Collaborate with External Auditors

- Engage third-party assurance providers to validate ESG data and enhance the credibility of disclosures.
- Ensure that auditors are familiar with relevant ESG frameworks and regulatory requirements.

4.5. Stay Informed About Regulatory Changes

- Monitor updates to ESG regulations and standards through industry groups, professional associations, and regulatory bodies.
- Provide ongoing training for finance teams to ensure they remain equipped to handle new compliance challenges.

Conclusion

Compliance and legal considerations are integral to ESG reporting, underscoring the need for finance professionals to take a proactive and strategic approach. By understanding the regulatory landscape, addressing key compliance challenges, and adopting best practices, finance professionals can help their organizations navigate the complexities of ESG reporting while minimizing legal risks. As the next chapter will explore, the fundamentals of ESG reporting go beyond compliance to offer a powerful framework for creating value and driving sustainable growth.

3

ESG Reporting Fundamentals for Finance

© 2024 Sekai FM | ESG for finance professionals

Section 1: Core Principles and Foundational Concepts

Environmental, Social, and Governance (ESG) reporting has evolved into a critical mechanism for measuring and communicating a company's impact on the environment, society, and its governance practices. For finance professionals, understanding the core principles and foundational concepts of ESG reporting is essential for producing accurate, credible, and actionable disclosures that meet regulatory requirements and stakeholder expectations. This section outlines the key principles that underpin ESG reporting and explains the foundational concepts that guide its practice.

1. Core Principles of ESG Reporting

Effective ESG reporting is built on a set of core principles that ensure the disclosures are meaningful, reliable, and aligned with stakeholder needs. These principles provide a framework for finance professionals to navigate the complexities of ESG reporting and deliver value through transparency and accountability.

1.1. Materiality - Materiality in ESG reporting refers to identifying and prioritizing the ESG factors that are most relevant to the organization's financial performance and stakeholder interests. Types of Materiality:

  - Financial Materiality: Focuses on ESG issues that impact a company's financial outcomes, such as regulatory risks or operational efficiencies. This perspective is emphasized in frameworks like SASB.
  - Double Materiality: Requires companies to disclose both the financial impact of ESG issues and their external impacts on the environment and society. This approach is central to the European Union's reporting standards, such as the CSRD.
- Implications for finance professionals: Conducting robust materiality assessments helps organizations focus their ESG efforts on areas that drive value creation while addressing stakeholder concerns.

1.2. Stakeholder Inclusiveness - ESG reporting should address the expectations and concerns of a wide range of stakeholders, including investors, employees, regulators, customers, and communities.

- Best Practices:
  - Engage stakeholders to identify their priorities and ensure that ESG disclosures are relevant and meaningful.
  - Align reporting with recognized frameworks, such as GRI, which emphasize stakeholder inclusiveness.
- Implications for finance professionals: Understanding stakeholder priorities enables finance professionals to craft ESG reports that build trust and enhance the organization's reputation.

<u>**Section 1: Core Principles and Foundational Concepts**</u>

1. Core Principles of ESG Reporting

1.3. Accuracy and Reliability

- Definition: ESG data must be accurate, complete, and verifiable to ensure the credibility of disclosures and prevent reputational or regulatory risks.
- Best Practices:
  - Establish rigorous data collection and validation processes.
  - Engage third-party assurance providers to enhance the reliability of ESG disclosures.
- Implications for finance professionals: finance professionals are responsible for implementing data governance practices that ensure the quality and integrity of ESG data.

1.4. Comparability

- Definition: ESG disclosures should allow stakeholders to compare performance across time periods, industries, and peers.
- Best Practices:
  - Use consistent metrics and methodologies for ESG reporting.
  - Align with global frameworks like SASB and TCFD to enhance comparability.
- Implications for finance professionals: Ensuring comparability enhances the decision-usefulness of ESG disclosures for investors and other stakeholders.

1.5. Transparency

- Definition: ESG reporting should provide clear and comprehensive information that enables stakeholders to understand an organization's sustainability efforts and performance.
- Best Practices:
  - Disclose both positive and negative ESG performance to demonstrate accountability.
  - Provide narrative context to explain trends and variances in ESG data.
- Implications for finance professionals: Transparent ESG reporting fosters trust and positions the organization as a leader in sustainability.

Section 1: Core Principles and Foundational Concepts

2. Foundational Concepts in ESG Reporting

In addition to core principles, finance professionals must understand several foundational concepts that shape the practice of ESG reporting. These concepts provide the theoretical and practical basis for integrating ESG into financial decision-making.

2.1. The Triple Bottom Line - The triple bottom line emphasizes measuring corporate performance across three dimensions: profit, people, and planet.

- Relevance to ESG Reporting: This concept underscores the interconnectedness of financial, social, and environmental outcomes, guiding organizations to adopt a more holistic approach to value creation.
- Implications for finance professionals: By incorporating the triple bottom line into financial analysis, professionals can provide a more comprehensive view of organizational performance.

2.2. Sustainability Context - ESG performance should be evaluated within the broader context of societal and environmental limits, such as global climate goals or regional biodiversity targets:

    - Align ESG goals with frameworks like the United Nations Sustainable Development Goals (SDGs).
    - Benchmark performance against industry peers and international standards.
- Implications for finance professionals: Incorporating sustainability context into ESG reporting enables organizations to demonstrate their contributions to global and regional priorities.

2.3. Integrated Reporting - Integrated reporting combines financial and non-financial information to provide a holistic view of an organization's performance and strategy.

- Relevance to ESG Reporting: Integrated reporting frameworks, such as the International Integrated Reporting Framework (<IR>), emphasize the role of ESG in long-term value creation.
- Implications for finance professionals: finance professionals play a key role in aligning ESG disclosures with financial statements, ensuring consistency and coherence across reporting outputs.

2.4. Dynamic Materiality - Dynamic materiality recognizes that the materiality of ESG factors can change over time due to shifts in stakeholder priorities, regulatory environments, or market conditions:

    - Regularly update materiality assessments to reflect evolving ESG risks and opportunities.
    - Monitor trends and engage stakeholders to anticipate emerging material issues.
- Implications for finance professionals: Staying ahead of dynamic materiality enables organizations to adapt their ESG strategies and maintain relevance in a changing environment.

Section 1: Core Principles and Foundational Concepts

3. The Role of finance professionals in Upholding ESG Principles

Finance professionals are uniquely positioned to uphold the principles and concepts of ESG reporting through their expertise in data analysis, risk management, and stakeholder communication. Key responsibilities include:

- Conducting Materiality Assessments: Identifying the ESG factors that are most relevant to financial performance and stakeholder priorities.
- Ensuring Data Quality: Implementing robust processes for collecting, validating, and verifying ESG data.
- Integrating ESG into Financial Reports: Aligning ESG disclosures with financial statements to provide a comprehensive view of performance.
- Engaging Stakeholders: Collaborating with sustainability teams, regulators, and investors to ensure that ESG reports meet diverse stakeholder needs.

By mastering the core principles and foundational concepts of ESG reporting, finance professionals can drive transparency, accountability, and value creation, positioning their organizations for long-term success.

Conclusion

The core principles and foundational concepts of ESG reporting form the bedrock of effective sustainability disclosures. For finance professionals, understanding and applying these principles is essential for navigating the complexities of ESG reporting, aligning with stakeholder expectations, and integrating sustainability into financial decision-making. The next section will delve into the metrics and indicators that bring these principles to life, offering practical guidance for measuring and reporting ESG performance.

Section 2: ESG Metrics and Indicators

Metrics and indicators are the backbone of ESG reporting, providing the quantitative and qualitative data that organizations use to measure and disclose their performance across Environmental, Social, and Governance dimensions. Understanding these metrics is essential for analyzing ESG performance, integrating it into financial reporting, and ensuring transparency for stakeholders. This section explores the key ESG metrics, their significance, and their application in corporate reporting.

1. The Importance of ESG Metrics

ESG metrics serve as the foundation for meaningful and actionable sustainability disclosures. They enable organizations to:

- Measure Performance: Metrics provide a standardized way to track progress on ESG goals, such as reducing greenhouse gas emissions or improving workplace diversity.
- Assess Risks and Opportunities: Quantifiable indicators help organizations evaluate how ESG factors impact financial performance and operational resilience.
- Enhance Transparency: Clear and consistent metrics build stakeholder trust by providing credible evidence of ESG commitments and achievements.
- Support Decision-Making: Investors and regulators use ESG metrics to evaluate an organization's sustainability performance and align capital allocation with long-term value creation.

ESG metrics are critical for integrating sustainability considerations into traditional financial analysis, bridging the gap between non-financial performance and financial outcomes.

2. Key ESG Metrics and Indicators

While ESG metrics vary by industry, geography, and regulatory requirements, there are widely recognized indicators that finance professionals should be familiar with. These metrics are often categorized by the three dimensions of ESG:

2.1. Environmental Metrics

Environmental metrics measure an organization's impact on natural ecosystems and its contribution to addressing environmental challenges such as climate change, resource depletion, and pollution.

- Carbon Emissions (Scope 1, 2, and 3)
- Biodiversity Impact
- Energy Efficiency
- Water Usage and Waste Management

Section 2: ESG Metrics and Indicators

2.1. Environmental Metrics

Carbon Emissions (Scope 1, 2, and 3)

- **Scope 1:** Direct emissions from owned or controlled operations.
- **Scope 2**: Indirect emissions from the generation of purchased electricity, heating, or cooling.
- **Scope 3:** Indirect emissions from the value chain, including suppliers and product use.

Carbon emissions metrics are critical for assessing regulatory risks, such as compliance with carbon pricing mechanisms, and evaluating the financial impact of transition strategies.

Biodiversity Impact

Indicators include the extent of land use changes, deforestation, and efforts to protect ecosystems.

Emerging Importance: Biodiversity metrics are becoming increasingly significant as regulators adopt frameworks like the Taskforce on Nature-related Financial Disclosures (TNFD).

Water Usage and Waste Management

Metrics such as water withdrawal intensity, waste recycling rates, and hazardous waste disposal practices reflect an organization's resource efficiency.

- **Implications**: Finance professionals use these metrics to assess operational risks, particularly in resource-intensive industries.

Energy Efficiency

Metrics include energy consumption per unit of production or revenue, and the percentage of energy sourced from renewables.

- **Relevance**: These indicators help quantify cost savings from energy efficiency initiatives and demonstrate alignment with global climate goals.

Section 2: ESG Metrics and Indicators

2. Social Metrics

Social metrics evaluate how an organization interacts with its employees, customers, communities, and other stakeholders, reflecting its commitment to ethical practices and societal well-being.

- Workforce Diversity and Inclusion: Metrics include gender and ethnic diversity at all organisational levels, pay equity ratios, and the representation of underrepresented groups.Diversity metrics influence investor confidence and reflect the organization's ability to attract and retain top talent.
- Employee Health and Safety: Indicators such as workplace injury rates, lost-time incident rates, and occupational health initiatives provide insight into employee well-being.These metrics are particularly important in industries with high health and safety risks, such as construction and manufacturing.
- Community Engagement: Metrics include investments in community programs, volunteer hours, and social impact initiatives.Community metrics can enhance brand value and reduce reputational risks associated with poor stakeholder relations.
- Human Rights Practices: Indicators such as the presence of modern slavery in supply chains and adherence to labor standards are critical for social responsibility.Increasing regulatory and investor scrutiny requires organizations to demonstrate strong human rights practices.

3. Governance Metrics

Governance metrics assess the structures, policies, and practices that guide an organization's leadership and decision-making.

- Board Composition and Independence: Metrics include the percentage of independent directors, board diversity, and the separation of CEO and Chair roles. (*Strong governance metrics reflect robust oversight and ethical leadership, factors critical to long-term financial stability*).
- Executive Compensation: Indicators include the alignment of executive pay with organizational performance and ESG targets. (*Transparent compensation practices build investor confidence and mitigate governance-related risks*).
- Anti-Corruption and Ethical Practices: Metrics such as the existence of anti-corruption policies, whistleblower protections, and compliance training programs reflect organizational integrity. (*Ethical practices reduce the risk of legal liabilities and reputational damage*).
- Transparency and Reporting Practices: Indicators include timely and comprehensive disclosures, alignment with global reporting standards, and third-party assurance of ESG data. (Transparent reporting enhances trust among investors, regulators, and other stakeholders).

Section 3: Data Collection and Management in ESG Reporting

High-quality data is the foundation of credible ESG reporting. Without reliable, accurate, and consistent data, organizations cannot effectively measure, analyze, or disclose their ESG performance. For finance professionals, the challenge lies in implementing robust systems and processes to collect, validate, and manage ESG data while ensuring its alignment with regulatory requirements and stakeholder expectations. This section provides an in-depth exploration of data collection and management in ESG reporting, offering practical insights and best practices.

1. The Importance of Data in ESG Reporting

Data plays a central role in ESG reporting, serving as the evidence that underpins an organization's sustainability disclosures. High-quality data is essential for:

- Ensuring Credibility: Accurate data enhances the reliability of ESG disclosures, reducing the risk of greenwashing or regulatory scrutiny.

- Enabling Comparability: Consistent data allows stakeholders to benchmark an organization's ESG performance against industry peers and historical trends.

- Supporting Decision-Making: Quantitative insights from ESG data guide strategic decisions, such as capital allocation, risk mitigation, and operational improvements.

- Meeting Regulatory Requirements: Increasingly stringent ESG regulations demand comprehensive and auditable data to demonstrate compliance.

For finance professionals, the ability to collect and manage ESG data effectively is a critical skill that aligns ESG performance with financial outcomes.

2. Key Challenges in ESG Data Collection and Management

Collecting and managing ESG data presents unique challenges, particularly for organizations with complex operations or global supply chains. finance professionals must navigate several obstacles, including:

2.1. Data Fragmentation
2.2. Lack of Standardization
2.3. Dynamic and Qualitative Metrics
2.4. Evolving Regulatory Requirements

Section 3: Data Collection and Management in ESG Reporting

2. Key Challenges in ESG Data Collection and Management

2.1. Data Fragmentation - ESG data often originates from diverse sources, including internal systems (e.g., HR or procurement data), external stakeholders (e.g., suppliers or community partners), and third-party assessments.

- Implications: Fragmented data increases the risk of inconsistencies and errors, making it difficult to produce comprehensive and accurate disclosures.

2.2. Lack of Standardization - Unlike financial data, ESG data lacks universally accepted standards for measurement and reporting, leading to variations in definitions, methodologies, and metrics across organizations.

- Implications: The absence of standardization complicates benchmarking and comparability, reducing the decision-usefulness of ESG data.

2.3. Dynamic and Qualitative Metrics - ESG data often includes qualitative or non-financial metrics, such as employee engagement or governance practices, which are more challenging to quantify and verify.

- Implications: Subjective metrics require additional context and narrative to ensure their relevance and reliability.

2.4. Evolving Regulatory Requirements - ESG regulations and reporting frameworks are evolving rapidly, requiring organizations to adapt their data collection practices to meet new standards.

- Implications: Keeping up with regulatory changes demands ongoing investments in data management systems and training for finance teams.

3. Best Practices for ESG Data Collection and Management

To address these challenges, finance professionals can adopt several best practices for collecting and managing ESG data:

3.1. Establish Robust Data Governance

- Definition: Data governance involves creating a structured framework for managing ESG data, including policies, procedures, and accountability mechanisms.
- Key Steps:
  - Assign ownership of ESG data to specific teams or individuals, such as sustainability officers or finance professionals.
  - Develop clear policies for data collection, validation, and storage to ensure consistency and accuracy.
  - Implement regular audits of ESG data to identify and address gaps or inconsistencies.

Section 3: Data Collection and Management in ESG Reporting

3.2. Leverage Technology for Data Management

- Advanced technologies, such as ESG data management platforms, enable organizations to streamline data collection and analysis.
- Key Tools:
  - Data Integration Platforms: Consolidate data from multiple sources into a centralized system, reducing fragmentation.
  - Analytics Software: Use tools like Tableau or Power BI to analyze ESG data and generate actionable insights.
  - Automation: Automate routine data collection tasks, such as tracking energy consumption or monitoring supply chain compliance, to improve efficiency and accuracy.

3.3. Align with Reporting Frameworks

- Aligning ESG data collection processes with established frameworks, such as GRI, SASB, or TCFD, ensures that the data meets stakeholder and regulatory expectations.
- Key Steps:
  - Map ESG metrics to the requirements of the chosen reporting framework.
  - Regularly review updates to frameworks to ensure ongoing compliance.
  - Engage with third-party consultants or auditors to validate alignment.

3.4. Engage Stakeholders in Data Collection

- Collaboration with internal and external stakeholders enhances the completeness and reliability of ESG data.
- Key Stakeholders:
  - Internal Teams: Work with HR, procurement, and operations teams to gather data on diversity, supply chain practices, and environmental performance.
  - Suppliers: Establish clear ESG data reporting expectations for suppliers, supported by training and audits.
  - Community Partners: Collect qualitative data on social initiatives through surveys, interviews, and third-party assessments.

3.5. Emphasize Materiality in Data Collection

- Focus data collection efforts on the ESG factors that are most material to the organization's operations, financial performance, and stakeholder interests.
- Key Steps:
  - Conduct materiality assessments to prioritize metrics that align with business goals and regulatory requirements.
  - Regularly update materiality assessments to reflect changing stakeholder priorities or market conditions.

Environmental Reporting

1. Key Environmental Indicators
2. Measuring and Reporting Environmental Impact
3. Best Practices in Environmental Disclosure
4. The Financial Implications of Environmental Reporting

Section 1: Key Environmental Indicators

Environmental reporting forms a critical pillar of ESG disclosures, addressing the ways in which an organization impacts and depends upon the natural environment. For finance professionals, understanding key environmental indicators is essential for evaluating environmental risks, identifying opportunities for operational efficiency, and ensuring compliance with regulatory standards. This section explores the most significant environmental indicators, their relevance, and how they are measured and reported.

1. The Importance of Environmental Indicators

Environmental indicators provide quantifiable data about an organization's interaction with the environment, enabling stakeholders to assess its sustainability performance. These indicators are critical for:

Compliance: Meeting regulatory requirements related to emissions, resource use, and waste management.

Risk Management: Identifying and mitigating environmental risks, such as climate-related disruptions or regulatory penalties.

Operational Efficiency: Tracking resource consumption and waste generation to identify cost-saving opportunities.

Investor Confidence: Demonstrating alignment with global climate goals & sustainability expectations enhances credibility with investors & stakeholders

Environmental indicators bridge the gap between operational practices and financial outcomes, allowing for a more holistic understanding of corporate performance.

2. Key Environmental Indicators

Environmental indicators vary depending on industry, geography, and stakeholder priorities. However, certain indicators are widely recognized as critical to effective environmental reporting.

2.1. Greenhouse Gas (GHG) Emissions
2.2. Energy Consumption
2.3. Water Usage and Management
2.4. Waste Generation and Management
2.5. Biodiversity and Ecosystem Impact

Section 1: Key Environmental Indicators

2. Key Environmental Indicators

2.1. Greenhouse Gas (GHG) Emissions - Measures the volume of greenhouse gases emitted by an organization, typically expressed in metric tons of carbon dioxide equivalent (CO_2e):

- Scope 1: Direct emissions from owned or controlled sources (e.g., fuel combustion in company-owned vehicles).
- Scope 2: Indirect emissions from the generation of purchased electricity, heating, or cooling.
- Scope 3: All other indirect emissions along the value chain, including supplier emissions and product end-use.

- Relevance: GHG emissions are central to climate-related risk assessments and regulatory compliance, such as carbon taxes or cap-and-trade systems.
- Measurement Standards: The GHG Protocol is the most widely used framework for measuring and reporting emissions.
- Implications for finance professionals: Accurate GHG reporting enables finance professionals to assess carbon-related risks, forecast costs associated with regulatory changes, and evaluate the financial benefits of decarbonization initiatives.

2.2. Energy Consumption

- Definition: Tracks the amount and sources of energy used by an organization, including electricity, natural gas, and renewable energy:
  - Total energy consumed (measured in kilowatt-hours or gigajoules).
  - Percentage of energy derived from renewable sources.
  - Energy intensity (e.g., energy consumed per unit of revenue or production).
- Relevance: Energy metrics reflect operational efficiency and provide insights into an organization's transition to renewable energy.
- Implications for finance professionals: Reducing energy consumption lowers operational costs and aligns the organization with global sustainability goals, such as net-zero commitments.

2.3. Water Usage and Management

- Definition: Measures the amount of water withdrawn, consumed, and discharged by an organization:
  - Total water withdrawn and consumed.
  - Water stress: The proportion of operations located in water-scarce regions.
  - Water discharge quality and compliance with local regulations.
- Relevance: Water is a critical resource for many industries, and inefficient usage or pollution can lead to regulatory penalties and reputational damage.
- Implications for finance professionals: Water-related metrics inform risk assessments, particularly for industries such as agriculture, manufacturing, and utilities, where water scarcity poses significant operational challenges.

Section 1: Key Environmental Indicators

2. Key Environmental Indicators

2.4. Waste Generation and Management

- Definition: Tracks the volume and type of waste produced, as well as methods of disposal or recycling:
- Key Metrics:
  - Total waste generated.
  - Percentage of waste recycled, reused, or diverted from landfills.
  - Hazardous waste disposal practices.
- Relevance: Waste metrics highlight resource efficiency and the environmental impact of production processes.
- Implications for finance professionals: Waste reduction initiatives can lower disposal costs and enhance the organization's environmental reputation.

3. Challenges in Measuring Environmental Indicators

While environmental indicators are critical, their measurement and reporting pose unique challenges:

- Data Availability and Quality: Collecting accurate data, particularly for Scope 3 emissions or biodiversity impacts, can be difficult due to reliance on external sources.
- Lack of Standardization: Variability in methodologies and definitions across industries complicates benchmarking and comparability.
- Dynamic Regulatory Landscape: Evolving environmental regulations require organizations to continuously adapt their measurement practices.
- Complex Value Chains: For multinational organizations, tracking environmental impacts across diverse geographies and suppliers is resource-intensive.

Financial professionals must address these challenges by implementing robust data collection systems, leveraging technology, and collaborating with sustainability teams.

Section 1: Key Environmental Indicators

4. Best Practices for Environmental Reporting

To overcome challenges and ensure effective environmental reporting, organizations should adopt the following best practices:

4.1. Align with Global Frameworks

- Use recognized standards, such as the GHG Protocol, GRI Standards, and TCFD Recommendations, to ensure consistency and credibility.

4.2. Invest in Technology

- Leverage data management platforms and analytics tools to streamline the collection, validation, and reporting of environmental data.

4.3. Focus on Materiality

- Prioritize environmental indicators that are most relevant to the organization's operations, industry, and stakeholder expectations.

4.4. Engage Stakeholders

- Collaborate with suppliers, community partners, and regulatory bodies to improve data quality and align reporting with stakeholder priorities.

4.5. Regularly Audit and Assure Data

- Conduct internal audits and seek third-party assurance to validate the accuracy and reliability of environmental disclosures.

Conclusion

Key environmental indicators provide the foundation for measuring and managing an organization's environmental performance. For finance professionals, mastering these metrics is essential for assessing risks, identifying opportunities, and supporting informed decision-making. In the next section, we will delve into methodologies for measuring and reporting environmental impacts, offering practical guidance for ensuring the accuracy and credibility of environmental disclosures.

Section 2: Measuring and Reporting Environmental Impact

Measuring and reporting environmental impact is one of the most critical components of ESG reporting, as it provides stakeholders with transparent and actionable insights into an organization's environmental footprint. For finance professionals, ensuring the accuracy and relevance of environmental disclosures is essential for compliance, risk assessment, and value creation. This section explores the methodologies, tools, and best practices for measuring and reporting environmental impact effectively.

1. The Importance of Measuring Environmental Impact
Environmental impact measurement forms the foundation of environmental reporting. It enables organizations to:

- Quantify Risks: Assess the financial and operational risks associated with climate change, resource depletion, and environmental regulations.
- Drive Strategic Decision-Making: Identify opportunities for cost savings, operational efficiencies, and innovation in sustainability practices.
- Ensure Compliance: Meet regulatory requirements and stakeholder expectations for transparency and accountability.
- Enhance Reputation: Demonstrate a commitment to sustainability, improving relationships with investors, customers, and other stakeholders.

Finance professionals play a pivotal role in ensuring that environmental impact measurements are robust, reliable, and aligned with both regulatory standards and strategic goals.

2. Key Methodologies for Measuring Environmental Impact
Accurate measurement of environmental impact requires standardized methodologies that ensure consistency, comparability, and credibility. The following methodologies are widely recognized and used across industries:

2.1. Greenhouse Gas (GHG) Emissions Measurement - the most widely used framework for calculating and reporting carbon emissions. It categorizes emissions into three scopes:

    - Scope 1: Direct emissions from owned or controlled sources.
    - Scope 2: Indirect emissions from purchased electricity, steam, heating, or cooling.
    - Scope 3: All other indirect emissions, including those from the supply chain and product use.
- Tools: Tools such as the Carbon Disclosure Project (CDP) and TCFD recommendations provide additional guidance for climate-related reporting.
- Challenges: Measuring Scope 3 emissions is particularly complex due to reliance on third-party data and supply chain transparency.

Section 2: Measuring and Reporting Environmental Impact

2. Key Methodologies for Measuring Environmental Impact

2.2. Life Cycle Assessment (LCA) - evaluates the environmental impact of a product or process across its entire lifecycle, from raw material extraction to disposal.

- Applications: Used to assess energy use, water consumption, and waste generation associated with specific products or services.
- Benefits for finance professionals: LCA provides detailed insights into environmental hotspots, enabling more targeted sustainability initiatives.

2.3. Water Footprinting

- Frameworks: The Water Footprint Network and ISO 14046 provide standards for measuring an organization's water footprint, including water use, consumption, and discharge.
- Relevance: Water footprinting is especially important for industries with high water dependency, such as agriculture, manufacturing, and energy production.
- Challenges: Accurately measuring water stress or scarcity across diverse geographic regions requires extensive data collection and analysis.

2.4. Environmental Impact Assessments (EIAs)

- Definition: EIAs evaluate the potential environmental effects of proposed projects, such as infrastructure development or industrial expansion.
- Applications: Used to assess risks to biodiversity, air and water quality, and community health.
- Benefits for finance professionals: EIAs support decision-making by identifying potential regulatory and reputational risks early in project planning.

Section 2: Measuring and Reporting Environmental Impact

3. Reporting Environmental Impact

Once environmental impacts have been measured, they must be disclosed in a clear, consistent, and transparent manner to meet stakeholder expectations and regulatory requirements. Effective environmental reporting involves several key steps:

3.1. Align with Reporting Frameworks

- Frameworks: Organizations should align their disclosures with globally recognized standards, such as:
  - Global Reporting Initiative (GRI): Focuses on sustainability impacts across environmental, social, and economic dimensions.
  - Sustainability Accounting Standards Board (SASB): Provides industry-specific guidance for material environmental issues.
  - Task Force on Climate-related Financial Disclosures (TCFD): Emphasizes the financial implications of climate risks and opportunities.
  - Integrated Reporting Framework (<IR>): Combines financial and non-financial information to provide a holistic view of organizational performance.
- Benefits: Using established frameworks ensures that environmental disclosures are comparable, credible, and aligned with stakeholder needs.

3.2. Structure Environmental Disclosures

- Key Elements to Include:
  - Baseline Data: Provide historical performance data to establish benchmarks and measure progress.
  - Key Metrics: Include metrics such as emissions intensity, energy efficiency, and waste reduction.
  - Targets and Goals: Clearly articulate short- and long-term environmental objectives, such as net-zero emissions or water-neutral operations.
  - Narrative Context: Explain trends, variances, and the actions being taken to address environmental challenges.
- Best Practices: Use visualizations, such as graphs and charts, to enhance the clarity and accessibility of disclosures.

3.3. Ensure Data Accuracy and Assurance

- Validation: Implement rigorous data validation processes to ensure the accuracy and reliability of environmental metrics.
- Third-Party Assurance: Engage external auditors or assurance providers to verify the credibility of environmental disclosures, reducing the risk of greenwashing.
- Technological Tools: Leverage data analytics platforms to streamline reporting and enhance data quality.

Section 2: Measuring and Reporting Environmental Impact

4. Challenges in Environmental Reporting

Despite its importance, environmental reporting presents significant challenges, including:

4.1. Data Gaps and Inconsistencies
- Many organizations face difficulties in collecting comprehensive environmental data, particularly for Scope 3 emissions or biodiversity impacts.

4.2. Evolving Standards
- The rapid evolution of reporting standards and regulatory requirements can make it challenging for organizations to stay compliant.

4.3. Balancing Transparency and Confidentiality
- While transparency is critical, organizations must also safeguard sensitive data, such as proprietary supply chain information.

4.4. Stakeholder Expectations
- Balancing the diverse expectations of investors, regulators, customers, and communities requires careful consideration of what to disclose and how.

Finance professionals must address these challenges by investing in robust reporting systems, staying informed about regulatory changes, and engaging stakeholders to ensure alignment.

5. The Role of finance professionals

Finance professionals are instrumental in ensuring the effectiveness of environmental reporting. Their responsibilities include:

- Integrating Environmental Metrics into Financial Reports: Align environmental performance data with financial disclosures, such as risk assessments and capital allocation decisions.
- Conducting Materiality Assessments: Identify the most relevant environmental metrics for the organization and prioritize their inclusion in reports.
- Engaging Stakeholders: Collaborate with sustainability teams, regulators, and investors to align reporting efforts with stakeholder expectations.
- Mitigating Risks: Use environmental data to identify and manage risks, such as regulatory penalties or reputational harm.

Conclusion

Measuring and reporting environmental impact is a critical component of ESG reporting, providing stakeholders with the information they need to assess an organization's sustainability performance. For finance professionals, mastering the methodologies and practices of environmental reporting is essential for driving transparency, compliance, and value creation. The next section will explore best practices in environmental disclosure, offering practical guidance for maximizing the impact and credibility of environmental reports.

Section 3: Best Practices in Environmental Disclosure

Environmental disclosure is a cornerstone of effective ESG reporting, providing stakeholders with transparent insights into an organization's environmental impact, risks, and mitigation strategies. For finance professionals, crafting credible and meaningful disclosures is crucial for regulatory compliance, investor confidence, and stakeholder engagement. This section outlines the best practices for producing high-quality environmental disclosures that align with global standards and meet the demands of a rapidly evolving regulatory landscape.

1. Principles of Effective Environmental Disclosure

High-quality environmental disclosures are guided by key principles that ensure transparency, relevance, and reliability. Finance professionals should adhere to these principles to produce reports that resonate with stakeholders:

- Materiality: Focus on environmental issues that are most relevant to the organization's operations, financial performance, and stakeholder concerns. For example, water usage is material for a beverage company but may be less relevant for a software firm.

- Accuracy: Disclosures must be accurate, verifiable, and free of errors or exaggerations to avoid accusations of greenwashing.

- Consistency: Maintain consistent methodologies and metrics across reporting periods to enable trend analysis and comparability.

- Transparency: Disclose both positive and negative environmental performance to provide a balanced and credible narrative.

- Forward-Looking Information: Include targets, strategies, and future commitments to demonstrate how the organization plans to address environmental challenges.

2. Components of Comprehensive Environmental Disclosure

Effective environmental disclosures typically include the following components:

2.1. Environmental Policy and Governance
2.2. Performance Metrics and Trends
2.3. Environmental Risks and Opportunities
2.4. Targets and Progress
2.5. Initiatives and Case Studies
2.6. Alignment with Global Goals

Section 3: Best Practices in Environmental Disclosure

2. Components of Comprehensive Environmental Disclosure

2.1. Environmental Policy and Governance:
What to Disclose: The organization's environmental policy, including commitments to sustainability and compliance with regulations. Governance structures overseeing environmental performance, such as the role of the board or a dedicated sustainability committee.
Best Practices: Highlight leadership accountability by detailing how environmental risks are integrated into overall corporate governance.

2.2. Performance Metrics and Trends
What to Disclose: Quantitative metrics such as greenhouse gas (GHG) emissions, energy use, water consumption, and waste generation. Year-over-year performance trends, benchmarks, and comparisons to industry peers.
Best Practices: Use visual aids (e.g., charts, graphs) to make data more accessible and engaging. Provide normalized metrics, such as emissions per unit of revenue, to contextualize performance.

2.3. Environmental Risks and Opportunities
What to Disclose: Key environmental risks, including regulatory changes, climate risks, and resource scarcity. Opportunities such as cost savings from energy efficiency or revenue potential from green products.
Best Practices: Align disclosures with recognized frameworks such as the Task Force on Climate-related Financial Disclosures (TCFD) to emphasize risk management and resilience.

2.4. Targets and Progress
What to Disclose: Short-, medium-, and long-term environmental targets, such as achieving net-zero emissions or transitioning to 100% renewable energy. Progress against these targets, including successes, challenges, and course corrections.
Best Practices: Ensure targets are specific, measurable, achievable, relevant, and time-bound (SMART). Disclose the methodologies used to track progress.

2.5. Initiatives and Case Studies
What to Disclose: Detailed descriptions of key environmental initiatives, such as renewable energy projects or waste reduction programs. Case studies highlighting successful projects and their outcomes.
Best Practices: Include qualitative narratives alongside quantitative data to illustrate the real-world impact of initiatives.

Section 3: Best Practices in Environmental Disclosure

3. Best Practices for Structuring Environmental Disclosures

The structure of environmental disclosures plays a significant role in their clarity and impact. Finance professionals should consider the following best practices:

3.1. Use a Standardized Framework - Align disclosures with established frameworks such as:

- Global Reporting Initiative (GRI): Focuses on broad sustainability impacts, including environmental performance.
- Sustainability Accounting Standards Board (SASB): Emphasizes industry-specific materiality.
- TCFD Recommendations: Focuses on climate-related risks and financial implications.

- Benefits: Ensures comparability, credibility, and compliance with stakeholder expectations.

3.2. Provide a Narrative Context - Pair quantitative data with qualitative explanations that provide context for trends, variances, and performance outcomes.

- Example: If emissions increased due to a one-time event, such as a facility expansion, explain this clearly in the disclosure.

3.3. Highlight Progress and Challenges - Be transparent about both achievements and areas where progress has been slower than anticipated.

- Best Practices: Use a balanced tone to build credibility and demonstrate a commitment to continuous improvement.

3.4. Leverage Digital Reporting Tools - Consider interactive online disclosures that allow stakeholders to explore environmental data dynamically.

- Benefits: Enhances engagement and accessibility, particularly for investors and analysts.

4. Challenges in Environmental Disclosure

Despite the best practices outlined above, environmental disclosure is not without its challenges:

4.1. Data Quality and Availability - Collecting accurate and complete data, particularly for Scope 3 emissions or biodiversity impacts, can be difficult.

4.2. Evolving Stakeholder Expectations - Stakeholders, including investors, regulators, and customers, have diverse and often conflicting expectations for environmental disclosures.

4.3. Balancing Transparency and Confidentiality - While transparency is critical, organizations must also protect sensitive or proprietary information, such as supplier data.

4.4. Resource Constraints - Effective environmental disclosure requires significant investments in systems, tools, and expertise, which may be challenging for smaller organizations.

Section 3: Best Practices in Environmental Disclosure

5. The Role of finance professionals in Environmental Disclosure

Finance professionals are integral to the success of environmental disclosures. Their responsibilities include:

Data Validation: Ensuring the accuracy, completeness, and reliability of environmental data.

Risk Assessment: Analyzing the financial implications of environmental risks and integrating them into broader corporate risk management frameworks.

Stakeholder Engagement: Collaborating with sustainability teams, investors, and regulators to align disclosures with stakeholder priorities

Continuous Improvement: Leveraging feedback from stakeholders and audits to enhance the quality and relevance of future disclosures.

Conclusion

High-quality environmental disclosures are essential for meeting regulatory requirements, building stakeholder trust, and driving sustainable business practices. By adhering to best practices and addressing common challenges, finance professionals can ensure that environmental reporting serves as a powerful tool for transparency, accountability, and strategic value creation. In the next chapter, we will explore the intricacies of social reporting, focusing on the metrics, methodologies, and practices that define this critical component of ESG reporting.

Section 4: The Financial Implications of Environmental Reporting

Environmental reporting is not only a regulatory requirement but also a strategic imperative with significant financial implications. For finance professionals, understanding how environmental factors affect financial performance, risk exposure, and investment decisions is essential for integrating sustainability into broader corporate strategies. This section examines the key financial implications of environmental reporting, highlighting its role in risk management, cost savings, access to capital, and long-term value creation.

1. Environmental Risks and Financial Performance

Environmental risks can have a profound impact on an organization's financial health. These risks are broadly categorized into two types:

1.1. Physical Risks - Risks arising from the direct physical impacts of climate change, such as extreme weather events, rising sea levels, and resource scarcity.e.g.

- Damage to physical assets from hurricanes or floods.
- Increased operational costs due to water scarcity in drought-prone regions.

- Financial Implications:
    - Higher insurance premiums or loss of insurability for assets in high-risk areas.
    - Disruption of supply chains and production, leading to revenue loss.
    - Devaluation of assets, particularly in industries like real estate and agriculture.

1.2. Transition Risks - Risks associated with the shift to a low-carbon economy, including regulatory changes, market shifts, and technological advancements. e.g.

- Carbon taxes or emission trading schemes that increase operating costs.
- Market demand declining for fossil fuel-based products.
- Costs of adopting cleaner technologies.

- Financial Implications:
    - Increased compliance costs to meet regulatory requirements.
    - Potential stranded assets in sectors reliant on fossil fuels.
    - Capital expenditure required to transition to renewable energy sources.

Finance professionals must quantify these risks and incorporate them into financial statements, scenario analyses, and risk management frameworks to provide a comprehensive view of the organization's exposure.

Section 4: The Financial Implications of Environmental Reporting

2. Cost Savings and Operational Efficiency

Environmental reporting often reveals opportunities to reduce costs and improve operational efficiency. Organizations that actively monitor and manage their environmental impact can realize financial benefits in the following areas:

2.1. Energy Efficiency - Reducing energy consumption through efficiency programs or transitioning to renewable energy sources.

- Financial Impact: Lower utility bills, reduced reliance on volatile energy markets, and potential tax incentives or subsidies for renewable energy use.

2.2. Waste Reduction - Implementing circular economy practices, such as recycling and reusing materials.

- Financial Impact: Decreased waste disposal costs and revenue opportunities from selling recycled materials.

2.3. Water Conservation - Reducing water usage in operations or improving water recycling systems.

- Financial Impact: Lower water procurement costs, reduced exposure to water scarcity risks, and compliance with regulatory standards.

2.4. Supply Chain Optimization - Partnering with sustainable suppliers or implementing green logistics practices.

- Financial Impact: Improved supply chain resilience and reduced costs associated with resource inefficiencies or regulatory non-compliance.

By integrating environmental considerations into operational decision-making, financial professionals can help organizations unlock cost-saving opportunities that align with sustainability goals.

Section 4: The Financial Implications of Environmental Reporting

3. Access to Capital and Investment Opportunities

Environmental performance is increasingly influencing investor decisions, making environmental reporting a critical factor in attracting capital and accessing new markets.

3.1. Investor Demand for ESG Transparency

- Trend: Institutional investors, such as pension funds and asset managers, are prioritizing ESG-integrated portfolios. Environmental disclosures help demonstrate a company's commitment to sustainability and resilience.
- Impact: Organizations with strong environmental performance and transparent reporting are more likely to attract investment and benefit from lower capital costs.

3.2. Green and Sustainable Finance

- Instruments: Green bonds, sustainability-linked loans, and other ESG-related financial instruments are growing in popularity.
- Benefits of Environmental Reporting:
    - Demonstrating alignment with green bond criteria or sustainability performance targets enhances eligibility for these instruments.
    - Accessing these markets can lower borrowing costs and improve financial flexibility.

3.3. Enhanced Credit Ratings

- Trend: Credit rating agencies are incorporating environmental risks into their assessments. Strong environmental reporting can lead to higher credit ratings, reducing borrowing costs.
- Example: Companies that disclose climate-related risks in line with TCFD recommendations may be viewed as better prepared for long-term challenges.

Section 4: The Financial Implications of Environmental Reporting

4 Reputational and Market Value Implications

A robust environmental reporting strategy can enhance an organization's reputation and market value, while poor performance or insufficient transparency can lead to significant financial repercussions.

4.1. Building Brand Equity

- Positive Impact: Transparent and credible environmental reporting demonstrates a commitment to sustainability, strengthening trust with consumers, investors, and other stakeholders.
- Example: Companies that lead in environmental initiatives, such as carbon neutrality or waste reduction, often achieve higher brand loyalty and customer retention.

4.2. Mitigating Reputational Risks

- Negative Impact: Environmental mismanagement, such as pollution incidents or greenwashing scandals, can lead to reputational damage, revenue loss, and shareholder activism.
- Example: Failure to disclose environmental risks transparently can attract regulatory scrutiny, litigation, or boycotts.

4.3. Competitive Advantage

- Organizations with strong environmental reporting can differentiate themselves in markets increasingly driven by sustainability criteria.
- Example: Companies that adopt sustainable practices early are better positioned to capture emerging market opportunities, such as demand for green products or services.

5. Long-Term Value Creation

Environmental reporting is a cornerstone of long-term value creation, enabling organizations to align sustainability with profitability. Key elements include:

- Future-Proofing Business Models: Identifying and adapting to environmental trends ensures that organizations remain competitive and resilient in a changing market landscape.
- Driving Innovation: Reporting on environmental challenges encourages innovation in products, processes, and technologies that align with sustainability goals.
- Engaging Stakeholders: Transparent environmental reporting fosters stronger relationships with investors, regulators, employees, and communities, building a foundation for sustainable growth.

Finance professionals play a crucial role in integrating these elements into corporate strategy, ensuring that environmental reporting is not just a compliance exercise but a driver of long-term success.

5

Social Reporting

1. Social Performance Metrics
2. Measuring and Validating Social Metrics
3. Best Practices in Social Disclosure
4. Financial Implications of Social Reporting

© 2024 Sekai FM | ESG for finance professionals

Section 1: Social Performance Metrics

Social performance metrics are critical components of ESG reporting, capturing how an organization interacts with its employees, customers, communities, and broader society. These metrics provide insights into an organization's commitment to ethical practices, inclusivity, and social responsibility. For finance professionals, understanding and integrating social metrics into reporting frameworks is essential for assessing risks, enhancing stakeholder trust, and aligning corporate strategy with long-term value creation. This section explores the key social performance metrics, their significance, and best practices for measuring and reporting them.

1. The Importance of Social Metrics

Social metrics measure an organization's impact on people - both internally, such as employees, and externally, such as communities and customers. These metrics are increasingly important because:

- Stakeholder Expectations: Employees, investors, customers, and regulators expect organizations to demonstrate a commitment to social equity and ethical practices.

- Operational Resilience: Positive social outcomes, such as employee satisfaction and community engagement, enhance operational stability and reduce reputational risks.

- Regulatory Compliance: Many jurisdictions require disclosures related to social factors, such as workforce diversity and human rights practices.

- Investor Decision-Making: Social metrics are integral to ESG-focused investment strategies, influencing capital allocation and shareholder engagement.

For finance professionals, social metrics provide a lens to evaluate non-financial risks and opportunities, enabling a more holistic view of corporate performance.

Section 1: Social Performance Metrics

2. Key Social Performance Metrics

Social metrics cover a broad spectrum of issues, from workforce diversity to community engagement. The most relevant metrics for ESG reporting can be grouped into three categories: workforce metrics, community impact metrics, and customer-related metrics.

2.1. Workforce Metrics

- Employee Health and Safety:
    - Metrics: Workplace injury rates, lost-time incident rates, and expenditures on health and safety programs.
    - Significance: Reflects an organization's commitment to creating a safe and supportive working environment. E.g. Reporting on progress toward achieving zero workplace injuries.
- Employee Engagement and Retention:
    - Metrics: Employee turnover rates, satisfaction survey results, and average tenure.
    - Significance: Indicates employee morale and the effectiveness of HR policies. E.g. Tracking improvements in employee engagement scores following the implementation of flexible working policies.

2.2. Community Impact Metrics

Community metrics evaluate how an organization interacts with and contributes to the communities in which it operates.

- Philanthropy and Volunteerism:
    - Metrics: Total monetary donations, employee volunteer hours, and community program participation rates.
    - Significance: Highlights an organization's role in supporting local communities and contributing to societal well-being. E.g. Reporting on the percentage of revenue allocated to charitable initiatives.
- Community Engagement: Participation in stakeholder consultations, partnerships with local organizations, and outcomes of community projects.
    - Significance: Demonstrates the organization's commitment to maintaining positive relationships with community stakeholders. E.g. Reporting on the impact of a community education program, such as improved literacy rates or graduation rates.
- Human Rights Practices: Policies and initiatives addressing modern slavery, labor rights, and ethical supply chain practices.
    - Significance: Mitigates reputational and regulatory risks associated with unethical practices. E.g. Publishing supplier audits to verify compliance with labor standards.

Section 1: Social Performance Metrics

2. Key Social Performance Metrics

2.3. Customer-Related Metrics
Customer metrics assess the organization's relationship with its customers, focusing on ethical practices, product quality, and customer satisfaction.

Customer Satisfaction

Metrics: Net Promoter Score (NPS), customer retention rates, and complaint resolution times.
Significance: Indicates the quality of the customer experience and brand loyalty.
Example: Reporting year-over-year improvements in customer satisfaction scores.

Data Privacy

Metrics: Number of data breaches, percentage of customer data encrypted, and expenditures on cybersecurity.
Significance: Addresses critical concerns about data protection and builds trust with customers and regulators.
Example: Disclosing compliance with global data protection standards.

Product Responsibility

Metrics: Product safety incidents, percentage of products certified as sustainable, and recall rates.
Significance: Demonstrates the organization's commitment to delivering safe, ethical, and sustainable products.
Example: Reporting on the lifecycle environmental impact of a flagship product.

3. Challenges in Measuring and Reporting Social Metrics

Despite their importance, social metrics present unique challenges for finance professionals:

3.1. Subjectivity and Qualitative Nature
Many social metrics, such as employee satisfaction or community engagement, rely on qualitative assessments or subjective data, making standardization difficult.

3.2. Data Collection Across Value Chains
Metrics such as supplier labor practices or product responsibility require data from third parties, often leading to gaps or inconsistencies.

3.3. Lack of Universal Standards
Unlike environmental metrics, social metrics lack universally accepted definitions or benchmarks, complicating comparability across organizations and industries.

3.4. Dynamic Stakeholder Expectations
Social priorities can shift rapidly, requiring organizations to adapt their reporting to address emerging concerns, such as workplace flexibility or mental health support.

4. Best Practices for Social Reporting

To overcome these challenges and ensure effective social reporting, organizations should adopt the following best practices:

- Conduct Materiality Assessments: Regularly evaluate which social metrics are most relevant to stakeholders and align reporting efforts accordingly.
- Use Established Frameworks: Align disclosures with recognized frameworks such as the Global Reporting Initiative (GRI) or Sustainability Accounting Standards Board (SASB) to ensure consistency and credibility.
- Integrate Stakeholder Feedback: Engage with employees, communities, and customers to identify areas of improvement and tailor reporting to their needs.
- Leverage Technology: Use data analytics and management platforms to streamline the collection and analysis of social performance data.
- Provide Narrative Context: Pair quantitative metrics with qualitative explanations to provide a balanced view of social performance.

5. The Role of finance professionals

Finance professionals play a pivotal role in social reporting by ensuring that social metrics are accurately measured, validated, and integrated into ESG disclosures. Their responsibilities include:

- Data Governance: Implementing robust systems for collecting and verifying social data, particularly from external sources such as suppliers or community partners.
- Risk Assessment: Identifying and quantifying the financial risks associated with poor social performance, such as labor disputes or data breaches.
- Stakeholder Communication: Presenting social performance data in a way that aligns with stakeholder priorities, building trust and engagement.
- Integration with Financial Reporting: Linking social metrics to financial outcomes, such as productivity improvements or reduced litigation risks, to provide a holistic view of corporate performance.

Conclusion

Social performance metrics are vital for assessing an organization's impact on people and addressing the growing demand for transparency and accountability. For finance professionals, mastering these metrics is essential for integrating social factors into ESG reporting, managing risks, and creating long-term value. The next section will delve into the methodologies and practices for collecting and validating social data, providing practical guidance for ensuring the quality and reliability of social disclosures.

Section 2: Measuring and Validating Social Metrics

Accurate measurement and validation of social metrics are essential to ensure the credibility of social reporting and align disclosures with stakeholder expectations. Social metrics, which often involve qualitative and human-centric factors, require robust methodologies to standardize data collection, assess performance, and demonstrate accountability. For financial professionals, understanding how to measure and validate these metrics is critical to integrating social performance into broader ESG frameworks. This section explores the key methodologies, challenges, and best practices for measuring and validating social metrics.

1. The Importance of Measuring Social Metrics

The measurement of social metrics provides organizations with the tools to:

- Assess Performance: Evaluate how well the organization meets its social objectives, such as workforce diversity or community impact.
- Manage Risks: Identify and mitigate risks related to social issues, such as labor disputes, reputational damage, or regulatory non-compliance.
- Enhance Transparency: Provide stakeholders with credible data that reflects the organization's commitment to social responsibility.
- Support Decision-Making: Use data-driven insights to guide resource allocation, improve employee engagement, and strengthen community relationships.

For financial professionals, measuring social metrics enables the quantification of non-financial risks and opportunities, linking them to financial outcomes such as cost savings, revenue growth, or reduced litigation exposure.

Section 2: Measuring and Validating Social Metrics

2. Key Methodologies for Measuring Social Metrics

Measuring social metrics involves both quantitative and qualitative approaches, often requiring a combination of primary data collection and secondary analysis. Below are some of the most widely used methodologies:

2.1. Surveys and Questionnaires - Used to gather data on employee engagement, customer satisfaction, or community perceptions.

- Example Metrics: Employee satisfaction scores, Net Promoter Scores (NPS), and stakeholder feedback ratings.
- Best Practices:
    - Ensure surveys are anonymous to encourage honest responses.
    - Use standardized scales to facilitate comparability over time and across groups.

2.2. Workforce Analytics - Tracks key workforce metrics, such as diversity ratios, pay equity, and employee turnover.

- Example Metrics: Percentage of women in leadership, turnover rates by demographic, and average pay by gender or ethnicity.
- Best Practices:
    - Integrate data from HR systems to streamline tracking.
    - Regularly benchmark metrics against industry peers to identify gaps and best practices.

2.3. Audits and Assessments - Independent audits of labor practices, supply chain operations, or human rights compliance.

- Example Metrics: Number of supplier audits completed, instances of labor violations, and corrective actions implemented.
- Best Practices:
    - Use third-party auditors to enhance credibility.
    - Develop clear criteria for assessing compliance and performance.

2.4. Community Impact Studies - Measures the outcomes of community programs, such as education initiatives, healthcare access, or infrastructure development.

- Example Metrics: Number of beneficiaries, improvements in literacy rates, or healthcare outcomes.
- Best Practices:
    - Collaborate with local organizations to ensure data accuracy and relevance.
    - Use baseline data to measure the incremental impact of programs.

2.5. Social Media and Public Sentiment Analysis - Tracks public sentiment and social media activity related to the organization's brand and social initiatives.

- Example Metrics: Sentiment scores, share of voice, and engagement rates.
- Best Practices:
    - Use advanced analytics tools, such as natural language processing, to analyze large datasets.
    - Monitor trends over time to identify emerging reputational risks.

Section 2: Measuring and Validating Social Metrics

3. Challenges in Measuring Social Metrics

Despite the importance of social metrics, their measurement presents unique challenges that require careful consideration and strategic approaches:

3.1. Subjectivity and Intangibility

- Many social metrics, such as employee engagement or community perceptions, are inherently subjective and difficult to quantify.
- Mitigation: Combine qualitative insights with quantitative data to provide a balanced perspective.

3.2. Data Fragmentation

- Social data often resides in disparate systems, such as HR platforms, community program databases, or supplier reports, leading to fragmentation and inconsistencies.
- Mitigation: Centralize data collection processes and standardize data formats to improve consistency.

3.3. Lack of Standardized Metrics

- Unlike environmental metrics, social metrics lack universally accepted standards, making it challenging to ensure comparability.
- Mitigation: Align metrics with established frameworks, such as GRI or SASB, to enhance standardization.

3.4. Data Gaps in Supply Chains

- Collecting data on social metrics from suppliers, particularly in global supply chains, is often difficult due to varying levels of transparency and capacity.
- Mitigation: Engage suppliers in capacity-building programs and conduct regular audits to improve data availability.

Section 2: Measuring and Validating Social Metrics

4. Best Practices for Validating Social Metrics

Validation is essential to ensure the accuracy and reliability of social metrics, particularly when they are used in external disclosures or decision-making processes. Financial professionals can adopt the following best practices for validation:

4.1. Data Verification

- Conduct internal reviews of social data to identify errors, inconsistencies, or outliers.
- Use cross-functional teams to validate data from different departments, such as HR, procurement, and community relations.

4.2. Third-Party Assurance

- Engage external auditors to verify key social metrics, such as diversity ratios or supplier compliance.
- Provide auditors with clear documentation and access to data sources to facilitate the assurance process.

4.3. Benchmarking

- Compare social metrics against industry standards or peer organizations to assess performance and identify areas for improvement.
- Use benchmarking to validate the relevance and accuracy of internally generated data.

4.4. Stakeholder Feedback

- Involve stakeholders, such as employees, community members, or investors, in the validation process to ensure metrics align with their expectations and experiences.
- Use stakeholder feedback to refine methodologies and improve data quality.

Section 2: Measuring and Validating Social Metrics

5. The Role of Technology in Measuring and Validating Social Metrics

Technology plays a critical role in streamlining the measurement and validation of social metrics. Key tools and systems include:

- HR Analytics Platforms: Track workforce metrics such as diversity, turnover, and pay equity in real time.
- Social Impact Measurement Tools: Evaluate the outcomes of community programs using specialized software, such as impact assessment platforms.
- Data Integration Systems: Centralize social data from multiple sources into a unified dashboard for easier analysis and reporting.
- Artificial Intelligence (AI): Use AI-powered tools to analyze large datasets, such as social media sentiment or employee surveys, for deeper insights.

By leveraging technology, financial professionals can enhance the efficiency and accuracy of social metric measurement and validation.

6. The Role of Financial Professionals

Financial professionals play a pivotal role in ensuring the quality and credibility of social metrics. Their responsibilities include:

- Designing Data Collection Processes: Develop robust workflows for gathering social data across departments and supply chains.
- Integrating Social Metrics into Reporting: Ensure that social data is seamlessly integrated into ESG reports and aligned with financial disclosures.
- Identifying Risks and Opportunities: Use social metrics to assess risks, such as labor disputes or reputational harm, and identify opportunities for value creation.
- Engaging Stakeholders: Communicate social performance data to stakeholders in a transparent and meaningful way.

Conclusion

Measuring and validating social metrics is a complex but essential aspect of ESG reporting. By adopting robust methodologies, addressing challenges, and leveraging technology, financial professionals can ensure the accuracy, relevance, and credibility of social disclosures. These efforts not only enhance transparency and accountability but also enable organizations to align their social performance with broader strategic objectives. The next section will explore best practices in social disclosure, focusing on how to effectively communicate social performance to stakeholders.

Section 3: Best Practices in Social Disclosure

Social disclosure is a vital component of ESG reporting, offering stakeholders transparency into how organizations address critical social issues such as employee well-being, diversity, community engagement, and ethical practices. For financial professionals, crafting high-quality social disclosures requires balancing regulatory compliance, stakeholder expectations, and the organization's strategic objectives. This section explores best practices for ensuring that social disclosures are accurate, meaningful, and aligned with global standards.

1. Principles of Effective Social Disclosure

High-quality social disclosures are guided by key principles that ensure they meet the needs of stakeholders while supporting organizational objectives:

1.1. Materiality

- Definition: Focus disclosures on the social issues that are most relevant to the organization's operations, financial performance, and stakeholder interests.
- Application: Conduct materiality assessments to identify priority areas, such as workforce diversity, labor practices, or community engagement, and tailor disclosures accordingly

1.2. Transparency

- Definition: Provide clear and comprehensive information about the organization's social performance, including both achievements and areas for improvement.
- Application: Avoid omitting or downplaying challenges, such as high employee turnover or unresolved labor disputes, to build credibility.

1.3. Consistency

- Definition: Use consistent metrics, methodologies, and reporting formats across reporting periods to enable trend analysis and comparability.
- Application: Align disclosures with established frameworks, such as the Global Reporting Initiative (GRI) or Sustainability Accounting Standards Board (SASB), to maintain consistency.

1.4. Stakeholder Relevance

- Definition: Address the concerns and priorities of key stakeholder groups, such as employees, investors, customers, and regulators.
- Application: Use stakeholder engagement processes to inform the scope and focus of social disclosures.

Section 3: Best Practices in Social Disclosure

2. Components of Comprehensive Social Disclosures

To create meaningful social disclosures, organizations should address key areas that align with stakeholder expectations and global reporting frameworks:

2.1. Workforce Practices

- What to Disclose:
    - Workforce demographics, including diversity metrics and representation of underrepresented groups.
    - Employee turnover rates, health and safety metrics, and training and development initiatives.
    - Pay equity analysis and measures to address wage gaps.
- Best Practices:
    - Use disaggregated data to highlight disparities across demographic groups.
    - Provide contextual information, such as progress toward workforce diversity goals or improvements in workplace safety.

2.2. Community Engagement

- What to Disclose:
    - Details of community programs, including objectives, funding, and measurable outcomes.
    - Partnerships with local organizations and government agencies to address community needs.
    - Stakeholder consultation processes and how community feedback has been incorporated into decision-making.
- Best Practices:
    - Highlight the alignment of community initiatives with global frameworks, such as the United Nations Sustainable Development Goals (SDGs).
    - Use case studies to illustrate the tangible impact of programs.

Section 3: Best Practices in Social Disclosure

2.3. Supply Chain Practices

- What to Disclose:
  - Ethical sourcing policies and supplier audits, including compliance with labor and human rights standards.
  - Measures to prevent modern slavery, forced labor, and child labor in the supply chain.
  - Supplier diversity programs and initiatives to support small and minority-owned businesses.
- Best Practices:
  - Provide data on the percentage of suppliers audited and the results of those audits.
  - Disclose remediation actions taken to address non-compliance.

2.4. Customer and Product Responsibility

- What to Disclose:
  - Data privacy and cybersecurity measures, including metrics on data breaches and resolution times.
  - Product safety incidents and recall statistics, along with steps taken to prevent future occurrences.
  - Accessibility and inclusivity of products and services for underserved or vulnerable populations.
- Best Practices:
  - Align disclosures with global standards, such as GDPR for data privacy or ISO standards for product safety.
  - Include forward-looking commitments, such as plans to improve accessibility or enhance data security.

Section 3: Best Practices in Social Disclosure

3. Communicating Social Disclosures Effectively
Crafting social disclosures is only part of the process; how they are communicated plays a critical role in their impact. Financial professionals should adopt the following best practices to enhance the effectiveness of social disclosures:

3.1. Use Clear and Engaging Formats

- Best Practices:
  - Present data visually using graphs, charts, and infographics to improve accessibility and engagement.
  - Use storytelling techniques to contextualize metrics with real-world examples or case studies.

3.2. Integrate Social Disclosures into Broader Reporting

- Best Practices:
  - Include social disclosures in integrated reports or standalone sustainability reports to provide a holistic view of ESG performance.
  - Ensure alignment between social metrics and other ESG components, such as governance or environmental disclosures.

3.3. Tailor Disclosures to Stakeholder Needs

- Best Practices:
  - Customize disclosures for different stakeholder groups, such as detailed metrics for investors or simplified narratives for community members.
  - Use digital platforms, such as interactive dashboards or online reports, to make disclosures more accessible.

4. Challenges in Social Disclosure
Despite best practices, organizations often face challenges in producing high-quality social disclosures:

4.1. Data Availability and Quality - Collecting reliable data, particularly from global supply chains or third-party sources, can be difficult.

- Mitigation: Invest in robust data management systems and engage suppliers in capacity-building programs.

4.2. Evolving Stakeholder Expectations - Social priorities, such as workplace flexibility or mental health support, can change rapidly.

- Mitigation: Use stakeholder engagement processes to stay informed about emerging concerns.

4.3. Regulatory Complexity - Navigating varying regulatory requirements across jurisdictions adds complexity to social disclosures.

- Mitigation: Align disclosures with international frameworks to create a unified reporting approach.

Section 3: Best Practices in Social Disclosure

5. The Role of Financial Professionals

Financial professionals are essential to the success of social disclosures, as they bring analytical rigor, risk management expertise, and stakeholder communication skills. Key responsibilities include:

- Data Validation: Ensure the accuracy and reliability of social metrics, particularly those used in external disclosures.
- Risk Assessment: Identify risks related to workforce practices, supply chains, or community engagement and incorporate them into broader risk management frameworks.
- Strategic Integration: Link social disclosures to financial outcomes, such as cost savings from reduced turnover or revenue growth from improved brand loyalty.
- Stakeholder Communication: Present social disclosures in a way that builds trust and aligns with stakeholder priorities.

Conclusion

Effective social disclosures are critical for building trust, managing risks, and demonstrating accountability in today's socially conscious marketplace. By adhering to best practices and addressing common challenges, financial professionals can ensure that social disclosures are accurate, transparent, and aligned with stakeholder expectations. The next chapter will explore governance reporting, focusing on the metrics, methodologies, and practices that underpin this essential aspect of ESG reporting.

Section 4: Financial Implications of Social Reporting

Social reporting is not merely a matter of compliance or stakeholder engagement; it has direct and far-reaching financial implications. Social factors such as workforce well-being, diversity, and ethical supply chain practices can significantly impact an organization's financial performance, operational resilience, and long-term value creation. For finance professionals, understanding these implications is critical for integrating social metrics into financial decision-making and corporate strategy. This section explores the key financial impacts of social reporting, highlighting its role in risk mitigation, cost management, revenue generation, and investor relations.

1. The Relationship Between Social Reporting and Financial Performance

Social reporting reflects how well an organization manages its relationships with employees, customers, communities, and suppliers. These relationships are not just qualitative considerations; they have measurable financial impacts. Key areas include:

1.1. Operational Efficiency

- Workforce Productivity: High levels of employee engagement and satisfaction, often disclosed through social reporting, are linked to lower absenteeism, reduced turnover, and higher productivity.
- Supply Chain Resilience: Ethical sourcing and strong supplier relationships, highlighted in social reports, can reduce disruptions and enhance operational stability.
- Example: Companies with robust employee retention strategies often incur lower recruitment and training costs, translating into significant cost savings.

1.2. Brand Value and Customer Loyalty

- Social reporting on issues such as diversity, equity, inclusion (DEI), and community engagement influences brand reputation and customer loyalty.
- Example: Consumers are more likely to support brands that demonstrate strong social responsibility, leading to increased market share and revenue growth.

1.3. Regulatory Compliance and Risk Mitigation

- Social reporting ensures transparency in compliance with labor laws, human rights standards, and workplace safety regulations, mitigating the risk of fines or legal actions.
- Example: Organizations with transparent labor practices are less likely to face costly litigation related to labor disputes or human rights violations.

Section 4: Financial Implications of Social Reporting

2. Social Reporting as a Tool for Risk Mitigation

Social risks - such as workforce dissatisfaction, supply chain disruptions, or reputational damage—can have significant financial repercussions. Social reporting serves as a critical risk management tool by providing early warning signals and demonstrating proactive measures to mitigate these risks.

2.1. Workforce-Related Risks

- Risks: High turnover, low engagement, workplace injuries, or discriminatory practices can lead to productivity losses, litigation costs, and reputational harm.
- Role of Social Reporting: Disclosing metrics such as turnover rates, diversity ratios, and health and safety data highlights areas of concern & allows organizations to implement corrective actions.

2.2. Supply Chain Risks

- Risks: Poor labor practices or human rights violations in the supply chain can result in regulatory penalties, boycotts, or disruptions.
- Role of Social Reporting: Supplier audits and compliance disclosures demonstrate due diligence and mitigate risks related to unethical practices

2.3. Reputational Risks

- Risks: Negative publicity surrounding labor disputes, poor DEI performance, or lack of community engagement can erode trust and impact financial performance.
- Role of Social Reporting: Transparent disclosures build stakeholder trust and protect against reputational damage.

3. Cost Management through Social Reporting

Effective social reporting can identify cost-saving opportunities, particularly in areas such as workforce management and supply chain operations:

3.1. Workforce Costs : e.g. Reporting on employee engagement and turnover metrics enables organizations to identify and address retention challenges, reducing recruitment and onboarding expenses.

- Impact: Companies with higher employee satisfaction scores often spend less on training and experience fewer productivity disruptions.

3.2. Supply Chain Costs e.g. Ethical sourcing programs, disclosed through social reports, often lead to stronger supplier relationships, reducing costs associated with supply chain disruptions or non-compliance penalties.

- Impact: Collaborative supplier partnerships result in cost efficiencies, such as bulk discounts or streamlined logistics.

Section 4: Financial Implications of Social Reporting

4. Revenue Generation and Market Opportunities

Social reporting is increasingly seen as a driver of revenue growth, particularly as consumers, investors, and partners prioritize organizations with strong social performance:

4.1. Attracting Socially Conscious Consumers

- *Trend*: Consumers are more likely to support brands that align with their values, such as inclusivity or community impact.
- Example: Retail companies that report on fair labor practices or sustainable product sourcing often attract a loyal customer base, boosting revenue.

4.2. Securing ESG-Linked Investments

- *Trend*: Investors are prioritizing ESG-integrated portfolios, with social factors playing a key role in investment decisions.
- Example: Companies with strong social performance metrics, such as workforce diversity or community engagement, are more likely to attract impact investors or qualify for sustainability-linked financing.

4.3. Winning Contracts and Partnerships

- *Trend*: Many government contracts and corporate partnerships now require disclosures on social factors, such as DEI or human rights compliance.
- Example: Organizations that meet these criteria through transparent social reporting gain a competitive advantage in securing contracts.

5. Attracting and Retaining Talent

Social reporting plays a pivotal role in shaping an organization's employer brand, influencing its ability to attract and retain top talent:

5.1. Talent Attraction

- *Trend*: Job seekers increasingly prioritize employers with strong social performance, such as diversity initiatives or community involvement.
- Example: Disclosures on DEI programs and employee benefits help organizations stand out in competitive labor markets.

5.2. Talent Retention

- *Trend*: Transparent reporting on employee engagement and workplace practices fosters trust and loyalty among existing employees.
- Example: Companies that disclose and act on employee feedback report higher retention rates and improved productivity.

Section 4: Financial Implications of Social Reporting

6. Investor Relations and Social Reporting

Social reporting is becoming a critical factor in investor relations, influencing how financial markets assess organizational performance and value:

6.1. Meeting Investor Expectations

- *Trend*: Institutional investors increasingly demand comprehensive ESG disclosures, including social metrics, to assess non-financial risks and opportunities. e.g. Asset managers often screen companies for labor practices, community impact, and DEI performance as part of their due diligence.

6.2. Enhancing Capital Access

- *Trend*: Transparent social reporting improves access to capital markets by aligning with the criteria of ESG-focused investors and lenders. e.g. companies with robust social performance metrics qualify for ESG-linked loans or green bonds, often at favorable rates.

6.3. Reducing Cost of Capital

- *Trend*: Strong social reporting reduces perceived risks, leading to improved credit ratings and lower borrowing costs. e.g. Companies that report on labor compliance and workplace safety may benefit from lower insurance premiums or bond yields.

7. The Role of finance professionals

Finance professionals play a critical role in leveraging social reporting to maximize financial benefits and minimize risks. Their responsibilities include:

- Integrating Social Metrics: Align social performance data with financial reports to provide a comprehensive view of organizational performance.
- Quantifying Risks and Opportunities: Use social metrics to assess financial risks, such as labor disputes, and identify opportunities for cost savings or revenue growth.
- Engaging Investors: Communicate the financial implications of social performance to investors, highlighting alignment with ESG priorities.
- Strategic Decision-Making: Use insights from social reporting to guide resource allocation, operational improvements, and stakeholder engagement strategies.

Conclusion

The financial implications of social reporting extend far beyond compliance, influencing risk management, cost efficiency, revenue generation, and investor relations. For finance professionals, mastering the integration of social metrics into corporate reporting is essential for aligning sustainability with profitability and creating long-term value. The next chapter will explore governance reporting, focusing on the metrics, practices, and standards that underpin effective corporate governance and its role in ESG reporting.

Governance Reporting

1. Governance Structures & Their Impact on ESG Reporting
2. Ethical Practices & Transparency in Governance Reporting
3. Governance Metrics and Indicators
4. Integrating Governance Reporting with ESG Performance

© 2024 Sekai FM | ESG for finance professionals

Section 1: Governance Structures and Their Impact on ESG Reporting

Governance reporting forms the foundation of an effective ESG framework, providing transparency into how an organization is structured, managed, and held accountable. Strong governance practices not only enhance corporate performance but also ensure the credibility of environmental and social disclosures, reducing risks and aligning corporate strategies with long-term value creation. This section explores the key components of governance structures, their impact on ESG performance, and the role of finance professionals in ensuring effective governance reporting.

1. The Importance of Governance in ESG Reporting

Governance is the "G" in ESG, and its role is pivotal in ensuring that environmental and social goals are achieved responsibly and sustainably. Governance sets the tone for the organization, influencing decision-making, risk management, and stakeholder relationships.

1.1. Linking Governance to ESG Performance

- Effective governance provides the oversight and accountability necessary to integrate ESG principles into corporate strategy and operations.
- Weak governance, on the other hand, can lead to failures in ethical practices, regulatory compliance, and stakeholder trust.

1.2. Enhancing Stakeholder Confidence

- Transparent governance structures and practices build trust among investors, regulators, employees, and other stakeholders.
- Governance reporting demonstrates a commitment to ethical leadership, accountability, and long-term value creation.

1.3. Regulatory and Market Drivers

- Governance disclosures are increasingly mandated by regulators and expected by investors.
- Initiatives such as the UK Corporate Governance Code, the OECD Principles of Corporate Governance, and the UN Principles for Responsible Investment (PRI) emphasize the importance of governance in achieving sustainable business practices.

2. Key Components of Governance Structures

An organization's governance structure encompasses its leadership, policies, and decision-making frameworks. These elements collectively determine how ESG objectives are managed and monitored.

Board Composition and Oversight

- **Definition**: The board of directors is responsible for overseeing the organization's strategy, risk management, and ESG performance.
- **Key Metrics:**
  - Diversity: Representation of minorities, & individuals with diverse expertise on the board.
  - Independence: Percentage of independent directors who are not affiliated with the organization.
  - Committees: Presence of specialized committees, such as ESG or audit committees, to oversee specific areas of governance.
- **Best Practices:**
  - Ensure board diversity to bring varied perspectives and reduce groupthink.
  - Establish clear roles and responsibilities for ESG oversight, supported by regular training on sustainability issues.

Executive Leadership and Accountability

- **Definition**: Executive leadership, including the CEO and senior management, drives the implementation of governance policies and ESG initiatives.
- **Key Metrics:**
  - Alignment of executive compensation with ESG performance goals.
  - Frequency of ESG performance updates provided to the board.
  - Accountability frameworks, such as annual ESG performance reviews.
- **Best Practices:**
  - Tie a portion of executive compensation to ESG performance metrics, such as emissions reductions or workforce diversity targets.
  - Foster a culture of accountability by requiring regular reporting on ESG progress.

Ethical Policies and Compliance

- **Definition**: Governance includes the development and enforcement of ethical policies to guide behavior, ensure compliance, and mitigate risks.
- **Key Metrics:**
  - Existence of codes of conduct and ethics policies.
  - Frequency of ethics training for employees and leadership.
  - Number of incidents related to ethical breaches or regulatory violations.
- **Best Practices:**
  - Regularly update codes of conduct to reflect emerging risks and regulatory changes.
  - Implement whistleblower mechanisms to encourage reporting of unethical behavior.

Risk Management Frameworks

- **Definition**: Governance structures are responsible for identifying, assessing, and mitigating risks, including ESG-related risks.
- **Key Metrics:**
  - Integration of ESG risks into enterprise risk management (ERM) frameworks.
  - Frequency of risk assessments, including scenario analysis for climate-related risks.
  - Use of internal audits to monitor governance and ESG compliance.
- **Best Practices:**
  - Align risk management practices with global frameworks, such as the Task Force on Climate-related Financial Disclosures (TCFD).
  - Regularly update risk registers to reflect evolving ESG risks and opportunities.

Section 1: Governance Structures and Their Impact on ESG Reporting

3. Challenges in Governance Reporting

Despite its importance, governance reporting poses several challenges for organisations, particularly as stakeholders demand greater transparency and accountability:

3.1. Fragmented Reporting Practices - Governance data often resides in different departments, making it difficult to present a unified narrative.

- *Solution*: Centralize governance reporting processes to ensure consistency and coherence.

3.2. Balancing Transparency with Confidentiality - Disclosing governance practices and decision-making processes can expose sensitive information.

- *Solution*: Strike a balance by focusing on high-level governance principles and practices rather than specific operational details.

3.3. Lack of Standardized Metrics - Governance metrics vary across industries and jurisdictions, complicating comparability and benchmarking.

- *Solution*: Align reporting with globally recognized frameworks, such as the GRI Standards or SASB Standards, to enhance comparability.

4. Best Practices for Governance Reporting

To address these challenges and maximize the impact of governance reporting, organizations should adopt the following best practices:

4.1. Align with Global Frameworks

- Use recognized governance reporting standards, such as:
    - Global Reporting Initiative (GRI): Provides guidance on disclosing governance practices and ethical policies.
    - Sustainability Accounting Standards Board (SASB): Offers industry-specific metrics for governance reporting.
    - OECD Principles of Corporate Governance: Emphasizes transparency, accountability, and stakeholder engagement.

4.2. Integrate ESG Oversight into Governance Structures

- Establish dedicated ESG committees or task forces to oversee sustainability initiatives and ensure alignment with corporate strategy.
- Regularly update the board and executive team on ESG performance and emerging risks.

4.3. Use Clear and Accessible Formats

- Present governance disclosures in a clear and structured format, using visual aids such as organizational charts or infographics to enhance understanding.
- Publish governance reports as standalone documents or integrate them into broader ESG or annual reports.

4.4. Enhance Stakeholder Engagement

- Solicit feedback from stakeholders, including investors, employees, and regulators, to refine governance practices and reporting.
- Disclose how stakeholder concerns have been addressed in governance decisions.

Section 1: Governance Structures and Their Impact on ESG Reporting

5. The Role of finance professionals in Governance Reporting

Finance professionals are integral to governance reporting, leveraging their expertise in data analysis, risk management, and stakeholder communication to ensure high-quality disclosures. Key responsibilities include:

- Data Collection and Validation: Centralize and validate governance data from across the organization to ensure accuracy and reliability.
- Risk Assessment: Analyze governance risks, such as executive accountability or board diversity gaps, and recommend mitigation strategies.
- Integration with ESG Reporting: Align governance disclosures with environmental and social metrics to provide a holistic view of organizational performance.
- Stakeholder Communication: Present governance reports in a way that builds trust and demonstrates accountability.

Conclusion

Governance structures are the backbone of effective ESG reporting, providing the oversight and accountability necessary to achieve sustainable business practices. By adhering to best practices and addressing challenges, organizations can ensure that governance reporting meets stakeholder expectations and enhances long-term value creation. The next section will delve into ethical practices and transparency in governance reporting, exploring how organizations can build trust and credibility through robust disclosures.

Section 2: Ethical Practices and Transparency in Governance Reporting

Ethical practices and transparency form the cornerstone of governance reporting, ensuring that organizations operate with integrity and accountability. These principles are fundamental not only for compliance but also for fostering trust among stakeholders and enhancing long-term value creation. This section explores the role of ethical practices in governance, the importance of transparency in reporting, and the tools and strategies organizations can use to uphold these principles effectively.

1. The Role of Ethical Practices in Governance

Ethical governance practices define the standards and principles that guide organizational behavior, decision-making, and stakeholder interactions. They ensure that organizations operate responsibly, mitigate risks, and uphold the trust of their stakeholders.

1.1. Defining Ethical Practices in Governance

Code of Ethics: *A formal document outlining the organization's values, ethical principles, and expected behaviors.*

Ethical Leadership: *Leaders who set the tone for ethical conduct through their actions, decisions, and communications.*

Whistleblower Protections: *Mechanisms to encourage reporting of unethical practices without fear of retaliation.*

1.2. Benefits of Ethical Governance

Risk Mitigation: *Reduces the likelihood of fraud, corruption, and regulatory violations.*

Reputation Management: *Builds a positive brand image and strengthens stakeholder trust.*

Operational Efficiency: *Creates a culture of accountability, enhancing employee engagement and productivity.*

Section 2: Ethical Practices and Transparency in Governance Reporting

2. Transparency in Governance Reporting

Transparency is a critical element of governance reporting, as it allows stakeholders to assess the organization's commitment to accountability and ethical behavior. Effective transparency involves clear, consistent, and accessible communication of governance practices, policies, and performance.

2.1 Dimensions of Transparency

Decision-Making Processes: *Disclosing how decisions are made at the board and executive levels.*
Executive Compensation: *Providing details on how executive pay aligns with performance and ESG goals.*
Risk Management: *Outlining governance frameworks for identifying & mitigating risks, including ESG-related risks.*

2.2. Benefits of Transparency

Investor Confidence: *Transparent disclosures help investors evaluate risks & opportunities, increasing access to capital.*
Regulatory Compliance: *Ensures adherence to governance standards and reduces the likelihood of penalties.*
Stakeholder Trust: *Enhances relationships with stakeholders by demonstrating accountability and responsiveness.*

3. Key Components of Ethical and Transparent Governance Reporting

To uphold ethical standards and ensure transparency, organizations should focus on the following key components in governance reporting:

3.1. Governance Policies

- What to Include:
  - Codes of conduct and ethics policies.
  - Anti-corruption and anti-bribery measures.
  - Conflict of interest policies and procedures.
- Best Practices:
  - Regularly update governance policies to reflect emerging risks and regulatory changes.

Disclose how these policies are enforced and monitored.

Section 2: Ethical Practices and Transparency in Governance Reporting

3. Key Components of Ethical and Transparent Governance Reporting

3.2. Board and Leadership Accountability

- What to Include:
  - Composition and diversity of the board of directors.
  - Roles and responsibilities of board committees, particularly those overseeing ESG issues.
  - Processes for evaluating board and executive performance.
- Best Practices:
  - Provide details on the criteria used to assess board effectiveness.
  - Highlight efforts to improve diversity and inclusion within leadership.

3.3. Executive Compensation

- What to Include:
  - Structure and components of executive pay, including fixed salaries, bonuses, and long-term incentives.
  - Linkages between compensation and ESG performance metrics.
- Best Practices:
  - Use clear and comparable metrics to demonstrate alignment between executive pay and organizational goals.
  - Disclose pay equity initiatives to address wage gaps within the organization.

3.4. Whistleblower Mechanisms

- What to Include:
  - Processes for reporting unethical behavior, including hotlines or online reporting systems.
  - Protections for whistleblowers and outcomes of reported cases.
- Best Practices:
  - Ensure whistleblower mechanisms are accessible to all employees, suppliers, and stakeholders.
  - Regularly review and improve these mechanisms based on feedback and best practices.

3.5. ESG Risk Management

- What to Include:
  - Integration of ESG risks into the organization's enterprise risk management (ERM) framework.
  - Governance frameworks for managing climate, social, and reputational risks.
- Best Practices:
  - Disclose how ESG risks are prioritized and addressed at the board level.
  - Provide case studies or examples of risk mitigation strategies in action.

Section 2: Ethical Practices and Transparency in Governance Reporting

4. Challenges in Upholding Ethical Practices and Transparency

Despite their importance, maintaining ethical practices and transparency in governance reporting poses several challenges:

4.1. Balancing Transparency and Confidentiality - Disclosing governance practices must not compromise sensitive information, such as competitive strategies or proprietary data.

- *Solution*: Focus on high-level principles and practices while safeguarding confidential details.

4.2. Complexity of Global Operations - Multinational organizations face varying regulatory requirements across jurisdictions, complicating governance reporting.

- *Solution*: Align reporting with global standards, such as the OECD Principles of Corporate Governance or GRI Standards, to create a consistent framework.

4.3. Evolving Stakeholder Expectations - Stakeholders increasingly demand detailed governance disclosures, including those related to ESG risks and opportunities.

- *Solution*: Engage stakeholders regularly to understand their priorities and tailor disclosures accordingly.

5. Tools and Strategies for Enhancing Ethical Practices and Transparency

Organizations can leverage several tools and strategies to strengthen ethical practices and transparency in governance reporting:

5.1. Governance Frameworks

- Adopt globally recognized governance frameworks, such as the OECD Principles of Corporate Governance, to guide practices and disclosures.

5.2. Technology and Analytics

- Use governance, risk, and compliance (GRC) platforms to monitor and report on governance metrics in real time.
- Leverage data analytics to assess the effectiveness of governance practices and identify areas for improvement.

5.3. Third-Party Audits

- Engage external auditors to validate governance disclosures and ensure alignment with best practices.
- Provide auditors with access to relevant documentation and data for comprehensive assessments.

5.4. Stakeholder Engagement

- Conduct regular stakeholder consultations to gather feedback on governance practices and disclosures.
- Use stakeholder insights to refine policies and enhance the relevance of governance reports.

Section 2: Ethical Practices and Transparency in Governance Reporting

6. The Role of Financial Professionals

Financial professionals are essential in upholding ethical practices and transparency in governance reporting. Their responsibilities include:

- Ensuring Data Integrity: Validate governance data to ensure accuracy and reliability in disclosures.
- Integrating Governance Metrics: Align governance reporting with broader ESG disclosures to provide a holistic view of organizational performance.
- Risk Assessment: Analyze governance risks, such as ethical breaches or lack of diversity, and recommend mitigation strategies.
- Communicating with Stakeholders: Present governance reports in a way that is clear, accessible, and aligned with stakeholder priorities.

Conclusion

Ethical practices and transparency are fundamental to governance reporting, shaping stakeholder trust and organizational resilience. By focusing on robust policies, accountability, and clear communication, organizations can demonstrate their commitment to responsible governance. For financial professionals, ensuring the integrity and impact of governance disclosures is essential for aligning corporate behavior with stakeholder expectations and long-term value creation. The next section will explore governance metrics and indicators, detailing how to measure and report governance performance effectively.

Section 3: Governance Metrics and Indicators

Governance metrics and indicators serve as measurable benchmarks to evaluate an organization's adherence to principles of accountability, transparency, and ethical practices. These metrics are increasingly scrutinized by investors, regulators, and other stakeholders, who seek assurances of robust governance structures that align with long-term value creation. For finance professionals, understanding and effectively reporting governance metrics is critical to integrating governance into the broader ESG framework. This section explores the key governance metrics, their significance, and best practices for their measurement and reporting.

1. The Importance of Governance Metrics

Governance metrics provide tangible evidence of an organization's commitment to responsible corporate management. They offer insights into:

- Board Accountability: Evaluating the structure, composition, and effectiveness of the board in overseeing corporate strategy and risks.
- Leadership Integrity: Demonstrating the alignment of executive behavior and compensation with organizational goals.
- Transparency: Ensuring clear communication of governance practices, policies, and performance to stakeholders.
- Risk Mitigation: Identifying and addressing governance-related risks, such as conflicts of interest or ethical breaches, that could impact financial and reputational performance.

For finance professionals, governance metrics also enable a clearer understanding of how governance practices impact financial performance, operational resilience, and ESG outcomes.

2. Key Governance Metrics and Indicators

Governance metrics are broadly categorized into several key areas that reflect the structure, oversight, and accountability mechanisms within an organization.

2.1. Board Composition and Effectiveness.

- Metrics:
  - Board Diversity: Proportion of women, minorities, and individuals from diverse professional backgrounds on the board.
  - Independence: Percentage of independent directors who are free from material relationships with the organization.
  - Board Tenure: Average tenure of board members, balancing institutional knowledge with fresh perspectives.
  - Attendance Rates: Frequency of attendance by directors at board and committee meetings.
- Significance:
  - Diverse and independent boards are better equipped to address complex challenges, mitigate groupthink, and represent stakeholder interests effectively.
  - High attendance rates signal active and engaged oversight.

Section 3: Governance Metrics and Indicators

3. Challenges in Measuring and Reporting Governance Metrics

Despite their importance, governance metrics present unique challenges in measurement and reporting:

3.1. Lack of Standardization

- Governance metrics vary widely across industries and jurisdictions, making it difficult to establish uniform benchmarks.
- *Solution*: Align governance reporting with global frameworks, such as the OECD Principles of Corporate Governance, GRI Standards, or SASB Standards.

3.2. Subjectivity in Metrics

- Metrics such as board effectiveness or leadership integrity are inherently qualitative, making them harder to measure objectively.
- *Solution*: Use surveys, stakeholder feedback, and external evaluations to supplement quantitative metrics with qualitative insights.

3.3. Limited Data Availability

- Governance data, particularly from private companies or across global supply chains, can be difficult to access.
- *Solution*: Establish robust data collection systems and collaborate with third-party providers to enhance transparency.

4. Best Practices for Measuring and Reporting Governance Metrics

To ensure the effectiveness and credibility of governance metrics, organizations should adopt the following best practices:

4.1. Align Metrics with Global Standards

- Use recognized frameworks such as:
  - Global Reporting Initiative (GRI): Provides comprehensive guidance on governance disclosures.
  - Task Force on Climate-related Financial Disclosures (TCFD): Focuses on integrating governance into risk management and climate-related reporting.

4.2. Conduct Regular Assessments

- Implement regular evaluations of board performance, ethical practices, and risk management frameworks to ensure alignment with organizational goals and stakeholder expectations.

4.3. Enhance Data Quality

- Centralize governance data collection using governance, risk, and compliance (GRC) platforms.
- Use third-party audits to validate governance metrics and enhance credibility.

4.4. Provide Contextual Narratives

- Accompany metrics with narratives that explain trends, variances, and actions taken to address governance challenges or enhance performance.

Section 3: Governance Metrics and Indicators

5. The Role of finance professionals in Governance Metrics

finance professionals play a critical role in measuring, analyzing, and reporting governance metrics. Their responsibilities include:

Continuous Improvement: Use insights from governance metrics to recommend improvements in governance practices and align them with long-term organizational goals.

Stakeholder Communication: Present governance metrics in a clear and accessible manner, tailored to the needs of investors, regulators, and other stakeholders.

Data Integration: Consolidate governance metrics with financial and ESG data to provide a holistic view of performance.

Risk Analysis: Use governance metrics to assess risks, such as board inefficiencies or ethical breaches, and recommend mitigation strategies.

Conclusion

Governance metrics and indicators are essential tools for assessing and communicating an organization's commitment to accountability, transparency, and ethical leadership. By adopting best practices and addressing common challenges, finance professionals can ensure that governance metrics not only meet stakeholder expectations but also drive long-term value creation. The next section will explore how governance reporting can be integrated with environmental and social disclosures to provide a comprehensive ESG narrative.

Section 4: Integrating Governance Reporting with ESG Performance

Integrating governance reporting with environmental and social (E and S) performance is critical for presenting a cohesive and credible ESG narrative. Governance serves as the foundation that supports the effective implementation and oversight of environmental and social initiatives, ensuring that these efforts are aligned with corporate strategy and stakeholder expectations. For finance professionals, this integration is essential to demonstrate how governance practices drive ESG performance and long-term value creation. This section explores the mechanisms for aligning governance reporting with ESG metrics, the challenges involved, and best practices for creating a unified ESG framework.

1. The Role of Governance in ESG Performance
Governance is the enabling framework that ensures environmental and social initiatives are executed effectively and responsibly. It connects strategy, oversight, and accountability across the organization.

1.1. Oversight and Accountability

- Governance structures, such as boards and executive committees, provide oversight of ESG priorities, ensuring that environmental and social goals are integrated into business strategies.
- Example: A board-level ESG committee can oversee climate strategy, workforce diversity, and supply chain ethics, ensuring accountability at the highest levels of leadership.

1.2. Policy Alignment

- Governance ensures that policies, such as codes of conduct, anti-corruption frameworks, and risk management protocols, support environmental and social objectives.
- Example: A governance framework might establish procurement policies requiring suppliers to adhere to environmental standards and labor rights.

1.3. Risk Management

- Effective governance integrates ESG risks into enterprise risk management (ERM) systems, ensuring that climate risks, social issues, and reputational concerns are identified, assessed, and mitigated.

Section 4: Integrating Governance Reporting with ESG Performance

2. Benefits of Integration

Combining governance reporting with environmental and social performance offers several benefits:

2.1. Enhanced Stakeholder Confidence

- Integrated reporting demonstrates transparency and coherence in addressing ESG issues, building trust with investors, regulators, and other stakeholders.
- Example: Reporting on how governance frameworks monitor greenhouse gas (GHG) reductions and diversity initiatives provides a holistic view of the organization's ESG commitments.

2.2. Improved Decision-Making

- Aligning governance with ESG performance enables data-driven decision-making, ensuring that resources are allocated effectively to achieve sustainability goals.
- Example: Linking executive compensation to ESG targets, such as emissions reductions or workforce equity, aligns leadership incentives with strategic priorities.

2.3. Competitive Advantage

- Organizations with integrated ESG reporting are better positioned to attract ESG-focused investors, comply with emerging regulations, and meet evolving stakeholder expectations.

Section 4: Integrating Governance Reporting with ESG Performance

3. Key Areas of Integration

To effectively integrate governance reporting with ESG performance, organizations should focus on the following key areas:

3.1. ESG Oversight Structures

- What to Report:
  - The role of the board and committees in overseeing ESG strategy.
  - Frequency of ESG-related discussions and decisions at board meetings.
- Best Practices:
  - Establish dedicated ESG or sustainability committees at the board level.
  - Provide regular ESG training for board members to enhance their understanding of sustainability issues.

3.2. ESG-Aligned Incentives

- What to Report:
  - The integration of ESG metrics into executive compensation and performance evaluations.
  - Examples of specific ESG targets tied to compensation, such as emissions reductions or supplier diversity.
- Best Practices:
  - Use measurable and time-bound ESG targets to ensure accountability.
  - Disclose the percentage of executive bonuses linked to ESG performance metrics.

3.3. Integrated Risk Management

- What to Report:
  - The incorporation of ESG risks into the organization's ERM framework.
  - Governance processes for identifying and mitigating climate risks, labor violations, or reputational damage.
- Best Practices:
  - Align risk disclosures with frameworks such as the Task Force on Climate-related Financial Disclosures (TCFD).
  - Use scenario analysis to evaluate the financial impact of ESG risks.

3.4. Stakeholder Engagement

- What to Report:
  - Processes for engaging stakeholders, including investors, employees, and communities, on governance and ESG issues.
  - Examples of how stakeholder feedback has influenced governance or ESG strategies.
- Best Practices:
  - Use stakeholder consultations to identify material ESG issues and align governance practices with stakeholder priorities.
  - Disclose how stakeholder input is incorporated into board-level decisions.

Section 4: Integrating Governance Reporting with ESG Performance

4. Challenges in Integration

While integrating governance reporting with ESG performance offers significant benefits, organizations often face challenges in achieving seamless alignment:

4.1. Data Silos - Governance, environmental, and social data are often managed by separate teams, leading to fragmented reporting.

- *Solution*: Centralize ESG data collection and reporting processes using integrated data management platforms.

4.2. Lack of Standardization - Variability in ESG reporting standards complicates efforts to align governance disclosures with environmental and social metrics.

- *Solution*: Use globally recognized frameworks, such as GRI, SASB, and TCFD, to create a unified reporting approach.

4.3. Limited Board Expertise - Board members may lack the expertise needed to oversee complex ESG issues effectively.

- *Solution*: Provide ESG training for board members and consider appointing directors with sustainability expertise.

4.4. Balancing Transparency and Confidentiality - Disclosing governance practices and ESG strategies can expose sensitive information or create legal risks.

- *Solution*: Focus on high-level principles and aggregated data while safeguarding competitive or confidential details.

5. Best Practices for Integration

To successfully integrate governance reporting with ESG performance, organizations should adopt the following best practices:

5.1. Align Reporting with Global Frameworks

- Use frameworks such as the International Integrated Reporting Framework (<IR>) to connect governance, environmental, and social performance in a unified narrative.

5.2. Create Cross-Functional ESG Teams

- Establish teams that include representatives from governance, sustainability, risk, and finance functions to ensure alignment and collaboration.

5.3. Link Governance Metrics to ESG Outcomes

- Clearly demonstrate how governance practices drive ESG performance, such as linking board oversight to emissions reductions or workforce equity improvements.

5.4. Use Digital Reporting Tools

- Leverage technology to integrate ESG data into centralized dashboards, enabling real-time monitoring and reporting of governance and ESG metrics.

5.5. Provide Clear and Engaging Disclosures

- Use visual aids, such as charts and infographics, to illustrate the connection between governance practices and ESG outcomes.
- Include case studies or examples to demonstrate the real-world impact of integrated governance and ESG strategies.

Section 4: Integrating Governance Reporting with ESG Performance

6. The Role of finance professionals

Finance professionals are essential to the integration of governance reporting with ESG performance. Their responsibilities include:

- Data Integration: Align governance, environmental, and social data within a unified reporting framework.
- Risk Analysis: Quantify the financial implications of governance-related ESG risks and opportunities.
- Performance Monitoring: Track the impact of governance practices on ESG outcomes, such as emissions reductions or community engagement.
- Stakeholder Communication: Present integrated governance and ESG performance data in a clear, credible, and stakeholder-focused manner.

Conclusion

Integrating governance reporting with ESG performance is essential for demonstrating accountability, driving transparency, and aligning corporate strategy with stakeholder expectations. By adopting best practices and addressing challenges, organizations can create a cohesive ESG narrative that highlights the role of governance in achieving sustainable business outcomes. The next chapter will explore tools and technologies that enable accurate and efficient ESG reporting, focusing on their application in governance, environmental, and social contexts.

Integrating ESG into Financial Reporting

© 2024 Sekai FM | ESG for finance professionals

Section 1: The Case for Aligning ESG and Financial Reporting

Integrating Environmental, Social, and Governance (ESG) factors into financial reporting is no longer optional - it is a strategic imperative driven by regulatory mandates, investor demands, and the increasing recognition of ESG's materiality to financial performance. For finance professionals, aligning ESG and financial reporting enables a holistic view of organizational value and risk, bridging the gap between sustainability and profitability. This section explores the rationale for integration, its benefits, and the foundational principles that guide the process.

1. The Rationale for ESG Integration in Financial Reporting

The traditional boundaries of financial reporting are expanding as stakeholders demand transparency on ESG factors that directly or indirectly influence financial outcomes. ESG integration addresses this evolving landscape by embedding sustainability considerations into financial disclosures.

1.1. ESG as a Material Driver of Financial Performance

- Environmental Factors: Climate change, resource scarcity, and energy efficiency directly impact costs, revenues, and long-term resilience.
  - Example: Companies in carbon-intensive industries face regulatory risks, such as carbon pricing, which materially affects their financial performance.
- Social Factors: Workforce diversity, community engagement, and customer satisfaction drive operational stability, brand value, and revenue growth.
  - Example: High employee turnover increases recruitment costs, while strong community relations enhance market access.
- Governance Factors: Board oversight, ethical practices, and transparency reduce risks of fraud, litigation, and reputational damage.
  - Example: Weak governance correlates with higher financial misstatements, undermining investor confidence.

1.2. Regulatory and Market Pressures

- Regulatory bodies are increasingly mandating ESG disclosures that align with financial reporting.
  - Example: The European Union's Corporate Sustainability Reporting Directive (CSRD) requires companies to disclose ESG data alongside financial performance, reflecting the principle of double materiality.
- Investors prioritize ESG-integrated reporting to assess non-financial risks that may affect financial performance.
  - Example: Asset managers representing trillions of dollars in investments, such as BlackRock, emphasize ESG integration in their stewardship guidelines.

Section 1: The Case for Aligning ESG and Financial Reporting

1. The Rationale for ESG Integration in Financial Reporting

1.3. Stakeholder Demands for Transparency

- Investors: Require ESG data to evaluate long-term risks and opportunities.
- Regulators: Demand standardized ESG disclosures to enhance market stability and comparability.
- Customers and Employees: Expect organizations to align financial performance with ethical and sustainable practices.

Integrating ESG into financial reporting satisfies these demands, fostering trust and ensuring relevance in a rapidly changing market.

2. Benefits of ESG Integration for Financial Reporting

Aligning ESG and financial reporting offers tangible benefits that extend across operational, strategic, and reputational dimensions:

2.1. Enhanced Decision-Making

- Risk Management: Integrated reporting enables organizations to identify and address ESG-related risks, such as supply chain vulnerabilities or climate impacts, more effectively.
- Strategic Planning: By quantifying ESG impacts, organizations can make informed decisions about investments, resource allocation, and market positioning.
    - Example: A company integrating ESG risks into financial forecasting may allocate capital to renewable energy projects to mitigate future regulatory costs.

2.2. Improved Access to Capital

- ESG integration signals resilience and foresight, attracting ESG-conscious investors and lenders.
    - Example: Companies with strong ESG reporting often qualify for sustainability-linked loans with favorable terms tied to achieving ESG targets.

2.3. Regulatory Compliance

- ESG integration simplifies compliance with emerging regulations that mandate the inclusion of ESG data in financial reports.
    - Example: Companies aligning with the Task Force on Climate-related Financial Disclosures (TCFD) are better prepared for climate-related reporting requirements.

2.4. Enhanced Stakeholder Trust

- Integrated ESG reporting demonstrates accountability and a commitment to long-term value creation, strengthening relationships with investors, customers, and employees.
    - Example: Transparent reporting on workforce diversity enhances employee retention and attracts socially conscious talent.

Section 1: The Case for Aligning ESG and Financial Reporting

3. Principles of ESG Integration in Financial Reporting

Successful integration of ESG factors into financial reporting requires adherence to foundational principles that ensure credibility, consistency, and relevance.

3.1. Materiality

- Definition: Focus on ESG factors that are financially material or materially affect stakeholders.
- Application: Conduct robust materiality assessments to identify and prioritize ESG issues most relevant to the organization's financial performance.
    - Example: For a logistics company, fuel efficiency and carbon emissions are likely to be material, whereas water usage may not be.

3.2. Consistency

- Definition: Use consistent methodologies and frameworks across reporting periods to enable comparability and trend analysis.
- Application: Align ESG reporting with established financial reporting standards, such as International Financial Reporting Standards (IFRS), and ESG frameworks like GRI or SASB.

3.3. Transparency

- Definition: Provide clear, comprehensive disclosures that allow stakeholders to understand the relationship between ESG factors and financial performance.
- Application: Use narratives and case studies to contextualize ESG data, explaining trends and variances in performance.

3.4. Reliability

- Definition: Ensure that ESG data is accurate, complete, and verifiable.
- Application: Implement rigorous data validation processes and seek third-party assurance to enhance the credibility of ESG disclosures.

3.5. Integration

- Definition: Embed ESG data into financial reporting processes, ensuring alignment with the organization's overall performance narrative.
- Application: Present ESG data alongside traditional financial metrics in management discussions, risk assessments, and forward-looking statements.

Section 1: The Case for Aligning ESG and Financial Reporting

4. The Role of finance professionals in ESG Integration

Finance professionals are pivotal to aligning ESG and financial reporting. Their responsibilities include:

4.1. Data Governance

- Develop robust systems for collecting, validating, and managing ESG data to ensure its accuracy and reliability.

4.2. Risk Assessment

- Incorporate ESG risks into financial risk management frameworks, quantifying their potential financial impacts.

4.3. Performance Analysis

- Analyze the interplay between ESG performance and financial outcomes, such as the cost implications of climate risks or the revenue potential of sustainable products.

4.4. Stakeholder Communication

- Present ESG data in a manner that resonates with stakeholders, emphasizing its relevance to financial performance and long-term strategy.

Conclusion

Integrating ESG factors into financial reporting is no longer optional—it is a necessity for organizations seeking to remain competitive, resilient, and transparent in a rapidly evolving market. By aligning ESG and financial performance, organizations can not only meet regulatory and stakeholder demands but also unlock strategic and financial opportunities. The next section will explore the challenges organizations face in ESG integration and practical solutions for overcoming them, providing a roadmap for effective implementation.

Section 2: Challenges and Solutions in ESG Integration

The integration of Environmental, Social, and Governance (ESG) factors into financial reporting is a complex yet essential undertaking for organizations aiming to meet regulatory requirements, investor expectations, and stakeholder demands. Despite its importance, ESG integration presents several challenges, ranging from data quality issues to the lack of standardized frameworks. This section explores these challenges in depth and offers practical solutions to enable organizations to seamlessly align ESG performance with financial disclosures.

1. Key Challenges in ESG Integration

1.1. Data Quality and Availability

- Challenge: ESG data often originates from disparate sources, including supply chains, operations, and external stakeholders, making it fragmented and inconsistent.
- Impact: Inaccurate or incomplete data undermines the reliability of ESG disclosures, leading to potential reputational and regulatory risks.
- Example: Measuring Scope 3 greenhouse gas (GHG) emissions requires detailed supplier data, which can be challenging to obtain or verify.

1.2. Lack of Standardization

- Challenge: The absence of universally accepted ESG reporting standards leads to inconsistencies in metrics and methodologies across industries and jurisdictions.
- Impact: Stakeholders struggle to compare ESG performance between organizations, reducing the decision-usefulness of disclosures.
- Example: Companies aligning with GRI may report differently from those following SASB, complicating cross-comparison.

1.3. Evolving Regulatory Landscape

- Challenge: Regulatory requirements for ESG reporting are rapidly evolving, with significant variations across regions.
- Impact: Organizations face difficulties staying compliant, particularly if they operate in multiple jurisdictions.
- Example: The European Union's Corporate Sustainability Reporting Directive (CSRD) requires double materiality reporting, while other regions emphasize financial materiality.

1.4. Integration with Financial Systems

- Challenge: ESG data is often siloed from traditional financial systems, making it difficult to integrate into financial reporting processes.
- Impact: Misalignment between ESG and financial data hampers the ability to produce a cohesive and unified report.
- Example: Sustainability teams may use standalone tools that are not compatible with enterprise resource planning (ERP) systems.

Section 2: Challenges and Solutions in ESG Integration

1. Key Challenges in ESG Integration

1.5. Assurance and Verification

- Challenge: Ensuring the accuracy and credibility of ESG disclosures requires robust assurance processes, which many organizations lack.
- Impact: Stakeholders may question the reliability of ESG data, reducing trust in the organization's reporting.
- Example: Without third-party assurance, claims about emissions reductions or diversity improvements may be viewed with skepticism.

1.6. Skills and Expertise Gaps

- Challenge: Integrating ESG into financial reporting requires cross-disciplinary expertise, including knowledge of sustainability, finance, and data analytics.
- Impact: A lack of skilled professionals hampers the organization's ability to align ESG and financial reporting effectively.
- Example: Finance professionals may struggle to quantify the financial impacts of ESG risks without adequate training.

2. Practical Solutions for ESG Integration

To overcome these challenges, organizations can adopt targeted strategies that enhance their ESG integration efforts and ensure the credibility of their reporting.

2.1. Establish Robust Data Governance

- Solution: Implement systems and processes to centralize ESG data collection, validation, and management.
- Key Steps:
  - Use integrated platforms to consolidate ESG and financial data from multiple sources.
  - Standardize data collection processes across departments and geographies.
- Benefits: Enhances data accuracy, consistency, and reliability.

2.2. Align with Global Frameworks

- Solution: Adopt widely recognized ESG reporting frameworks to ensure comparability and standardization.
- Key Frameworks:
  - GRI: Focuses on sustainability impacts across all ESG dimensions.
  - SASB: Emphasizes financial materiality and industry-specific metrics.
  - TCFD: Provides guidance on climate-related financial disclosures.
- Benefits: Facilitates stakeholder understanding and ensures compliance with evolving regulations.

Section 2: Challenges and Solutions in ESG Integration

2. Practical Solutions for ESG Integration

2.3. Monitor Regulatory Developments

- *Solution*: Establish a dedicated team or function to track and respond to changes in ESG reporting regulations.
- Key Steps:
    - Regularly review updates from regulatory bodies such as the EU, SEC, or IFRS Foundation.
    - Engage with industry associations to stay ahead of emerging standards.
- Benefits: Minimizes compliance risks and ensures alignment with regulatory expectations.

2.4. Integrate ESG into Financial Systems

- *Solution*: Embed ESG data into existing financial systems, such as ERP or performance management platforms.
- Key Steps:
    - Develop cross-functional collaboration between finance, sustainability, and IT teams.
    - Use advanced analytics tools to link ESG metrics with financial performance indicators.
- Benefits: Streamlines reporting processes and enables holistic performance analysis.

2.5. Seek Third-Party Assurance

- *Solution*: Engage external auditors to verify ESG disclosures and enhance their credibility.
- Key Steps:
    - Define the scope and criteria for assurance, focusing on material ESG metrics.
    - Use assurance providers with expertise in both sustainability and financial reporting.
- Benefits: Builds stakeholder trust and reduces the risk of reputational damage.

2.6. Build Internal Capabilities

- *Solution*: Invest in training and capacity-building programs to enhance ESG expertise across the organization.
- Key Steps:
    - Provide cross-training for finance professionals on ESG principles and frameworks.
    - Develop specialized ESG roles within finance and sustainability teams.
- Benefits: Strengthens the organization's ability to integrate ESG into financial reporting effectively.

Section 2: Challenges and Solutions in ESG Integration

3.The Role of Technology in Addressing ESG Integration Challenges

Technology plays a pivotal role in overcoming the challenges associated with ESG integration. Key tools and systems include:

3.1. ESG Data Management Platforms

- Enable centralized data collection and validation across multiple sources.
- Facilitate real-time monitoring of ESG performance metrics.

3.2. Advanced Analytics Tools

- Use machine learning and data visualization to analyze ESG trends and their financial impacts.
- Provide actionable insights for decision-making and reporting.

3.3. Blockchain for Transparency

- Enhance the traceability and integrity of ESG data, particularly in supply chain reporting.

4. The Role of finance professionals

Finance professionals are essential to overcoming ESG integration challenges by applying their expertise in data analysis, risk management, and reporting. Their responsibilities include:

4.1. Data Validation

- Ensure the accuracy and consistency of ESG data across reporting periods.

4.2. Risk Analysis

- Quantify the financial impacts of ESG risks and develop mitigation strategies.

4.3. Stakeholder Engagement

- Communicate ESG integration efforts to stakeholders, emphasizing the link between ESG performance and financial outcomes.

4.4. Continuous Improvement

- Identify areas for improvement in ESG reporting processes and implement best practices.

Conclusion

Integrating ESG into financial reporting is a challenging but necessary endeavor for organizations aiming to align sustainability with financial performance. By addressing challenges such as data quality, standardization, and regulatory complexity through robust governance, technology, and capacity-building efforts, organizations can produce credible and actionable ESG disclosures. The next section will delve into case studies of successful ESG integration, providing practical insights and lessons learned from leading organizations.

Section 3: Case Studies of Successful ESG Integration

Real-world examples of successful ESG integration into financial reporting illustrate the strategies, challenges, and benefits organizations experience when aligning sustainability performance with financial disclosures. These case studies highlight how leading companies leverage governance, technology, and stakeholder engagement to create robust ESG reporting frameworks. This section examines three case studies, offering insights into best practices and lessons learned for finance professionals aiming to enhance their organization's ESG reporting.

1. Case Study: Microsoft – Aligning ESG with Financial Strategy

Microsoft is widely recognized for its comprehensive integration of ESG considerations into its financial strategy and reporting. The company's approach reflects a strong alignment between its environmental and social initiatives and its core business objectives.

Key Practices

- Carbon Neutrality Commitments: Microsoft integrates its carbon reduction targets into its financial disclosures by quantifying the costs of renewable energy investments and carbon offset purchases.
- Sustainability-Linked Financial Products: The company issues green bonds to fund environmental projects, linking its financing strategy to its sustainability goals.
- Transparent ESG Reporting: Microsoft's annual sustainability report aligns with frameworks such as GRI, SASB, and TCFD, offering stakeholders a clear view of its ESG impact.

Outcomes,Lessons for finance professionals

- Improved stakeholder confidence due to transparent ESG disclosures.
- Strengthened brand reputation as a leader in sustainability.
- Access to lower-cost capital through green bonds.
- Quantify the financial impacts of ESG initiatives to align them with broader financial reporting frameworks.
- Leverage sustainability-linked financial instruments to demonstrate a commitment to ESG goals.

Section 3: Case Studies of Successful ESG Integration

2. Case Study: Unilever – Embedding ESG into Decision-Making

Unilever has integrated ESG considerations into its financial reporting & operational decision-making, positioning sustainability as a key driver of its long-term strategy by:

- Sustainable Living Plan: Unilever's comprehensive ESG strategy focuses on reducing environmental impact, improving health and well-being, and enhancing livelihoods. These objectives are tied directly to financial performance metrics.
- Integrated Reporting: The company produces an integrated annual report that combines financial and ESG data, offering stakeholders a holistic view of its performance.
- ESG-Aligned Incentives: Unilever ties executive compensation to key ESG metrics, such as carbon reduction and water usage efficiency, ensuring accountability at the leadership level.

Outcomes,Lessons for finance professionals

- Enhanced operational efficiency through resource conservation initiatives, resulting in cost savings.
- Increased investor interest due to the alignment of ESG goals with financial performance.
- Improved employee engagement and retention by demonstrating a commitment to social and environmental values.
- Embed ESG metrics into incentive structures to align leadership behavior with sustainability objectives.
- Use integrated reporting to provide a comprehensive narrative of financial and ESG performance.

3. Case Study: Patagonia – Prioritizing Social and Environmental Impact

Patagonia, an outdoor apparel company, has built its business model around sustainability and social responsibility, making ESG integration a core aspect of its financial and operational strategy. Key practices are:

- Environmental Transparency: Patagonia discloses detailed information on its carbon footprint, supply chain practices, and product lifecycle impacts, linking these disclosures to its financial reports.
- Circular Economy Initiatives: The company invests in programs to repair and recycle products, reducing waste and extending product lifecycles. These initiatives are quantified and reported as part of its ESG impact.
- Community Investments: Patagonia allocates a percentage of its profits to environmental activism and community projects, reporting the financial and social outcomes of these investments.

Outcomes

- Increased customer loyalty and revenue growth due to strong alignment with consumer values.
- Reduced operational costs through waste minimization and resource efficiency.
- Recognition as a sustainability leader, attracting ESG-focused investors.

Lessons for finance professionals

- Quantify the financial benefits of sustainability initiatives, such as cost savings and revenue growth, to enhance the credibility of ESG disclosures.
- Use ESG reporting to build trust and loyalty among customers and other stakeholders.

Section 3: Case Studies of Successful ESG Integration

4. Cross-Cutting Lessons for ESG Integration

Across these case studies, several common themes and lessons emerge for finance professionals:

4.1. Align ESG Metrics with Business Strategy
- Successful ESG integration requires linking sustainability initiatives to business objectives, such as cost savings, revenue growth, or risk mitigation.

4.2. Use Recognized Frameworks
- Aligning ESG reporting with global standards, such as GRI, SASB, and TCFD, ensures transparency and comparability, enhancing stakeholder confidence.

4.3. Leverage Technology for Data Management
- Technology platforms enable efficient data collection, analysis, and reporting, bridging the gap between ESG and financial performance.

4.4. Engage Stakeholders
- Proactive engagement with investors, employees, and customers ensures that ESG priorities align with stakeholder expectations, building trust and credibility.

4.5. Provide Clear and Quantifiable Disclosures
- Quantify the financial impacts of ESG initiatives, such as cost savings from energy efficiency or revenue growth from sustainable products, to create a compelling narrative.

5. The Role of finance professionals

In each case, finance professionals played a critical role in integrating ESG into financial reporting. Their contributions included:
- Data Integration: Aligning ESG and financial data to create cohesive reports.
- Performance Analysis: Quantifying the financial impacts of ESG initiatives and demonstrating their value to stakeholders.
- Risk Management: Identifying ESG-related risks and embedding them into enterprise risk management frameworks.
- Stakeholder Communication: Crafting clear and transparent disclosures that resonate with diverse audiences.

Conclusion

The case studies of Microsoft, Unilever, and Patagonia demonstrate the tangible benefits of integrating ESG into financial reporting, from enhanced stakeholder trust to improved financial performance. By adopting best practices such as aligning ESG metrics with business strategy, leveraging technology, and engaging stakeholders, organizations can create robust ESG reporting frameworks that drive long-term value. The next section will explore tools and technologies that enable accurate and efficient ESG integration, providing actionable insights for finance professionals.

Section 4: Practical Frameworks and Approaches for ESG Integration

Effectively integrating Environmental, Social, and Governance (ESG) factors into financial reporting requires robust frameworks and approaches that align sustainability metrics with traditional financial disclosures. These frameworks guide organizations in standardizing ESG data, addressing stakeholder expectations, and navigating the complexities of evolving regulations. For finance professionals, understanding and applying these methodologies is critical to creating cohesive, transparent, and actionable reports. This section explores leading ESG integration frameworks, their applications, and how organizations can implement them effectively.

1. Importance of Frameworks in ESG Integration

Frameworks serve as the foundation for integrating ESG factors into financial reporting by offering standardized methodologies for data collection, analysis, and disclosure. Their importance lies in:

1.1. Ensuring Consistency and Comparability
- Frameworks standardize ESG metrics across industries and geographies, enabling stakeholders to compare performance and make informed decisions.
- Example: Investors can benchmark an organization's carbon emissions or board diversity against its peers.

1.2. Enhancing Credibility and Transparency
- Frameworks provide a structured approach to reporting, ensuring disclosures are accurate, verifiable, and aligned with stakeholder expectations.

1.3. Meeting Regulatory Requirements
- Adopting recognized frameworks ensures compliance with evolving ESG regulations, such as the EU's Corporate Sustainability Reporting Directive.

2. Leading Frameworks for ESG Integration

Organizations can choose from several widely recognized frameworks to align ESG and financial reporting. Each framework offers unique strengths tailored to specific needs and priorities.

2.1. Global Reporting Initiative (GRI) : GRI provides comprehensive standards for reporting on a wide range of ESG topics, emphasizing impacts on stakeholders and the environment. Key Features:
  - Focuses on double materiality, addressing both financial and non-financial impacts. Also encourages organizations to disclose sector-specific and cross-cutting ESG metrics.
- Applications:
  - Useful for organizations seeking to highlight their broader social and environmental impacts. Often paired with other frameworks, such as SASB or TCFD, for a more comprehensive approach.

Section 4: Practical Frameworks and Approaches for ESG Integration

2. Leading Frameworks for ESG Integration

2.2. Sustainability Accounting Standards Board (SASB)

- Overview: SASB focuses on financially material ESG factors, offering industry-specific standards that connect ESG metrics to business performance:
    - Provides detailed guidance for 77 industries, identifying the most relevant ESG issues for each.
    - Emphasizes the integration of ESG data into traditional financial reporting.
- Applications:
    - Ideal for organizations aiming to link ESG performance with financial outcomes, such as cost savings or risk mitigation.

2.3. Task Force on Climate-related Financial Disclosures (TCFD)

- Overview: TCFD provides guidance on disclosing climate-related risks and opportunities, emphasizing their financial implications:
    - Focuses on governance, strategy, risk management, and metrics for climate-related reporting.
    - Encourages scenario analysis to assess the impact of climate risks under different temperature pathways.
- Applications:
    - Particularly relevant for organizations in carbon-intensive industries or those exposed to significant climate risks.

2.4. Integrated Reporting Framework (<IR>)

- Overview: The Integrated Reporting Framework aims to create a cohesive narrative that combines financial and non-financial data:
    - Focuses on value creation over the short, medium, and long term.
    - Encourages organizations to connect ESG factors with financial performance and strategy.
- Applications:
    - Suitable for organizations seeking to present a unified report that aligns sustainability with overall business strategy.

2.5. Science-Based Targets initiative (SBTi)

- Overview: SBTi provides a framework for setting and validating emissions reduction targets in line with climate science:
    - Aligns corporate targets with the Paris Agreement's goal of limiting global warming to 1.5°C or well below 2°C.
    - Offers sector-specific guidance for industries such as energy, manufacturing, and transportation.
- Applications:
    - Useful for organizations aiming to demonstrate climate leadership and integrate emissions data into financial disclosures.

Section 4: Practical Frameworks and Approaches for ESG Integration

3. Steps to Implement ESG Integration Frameworks

Successful implementation of ESG frameworks requires a structured and collaborative approach. Key steps include:

3.1. Conduct a Materiality Assessment

- Purpose: Identify the ESG factors that are most relevant to the organization's financial performance and stakeholder priorities.
- Key Actions:
  - Engage stakeholders, including investors, employees, and customers, to understand their expectations.
  - Use tools such as surveys, workshops, and external benchmarks to prioritize ESG issues.

3.2. Establish Governance and Oversight

- Purpose: Ensure accountability and alignment of ESG efforts across the organization.
- Key Actions:
  - Assign responsibility for ESG reporting to a dedicated committee or cross-functional team.
  - Integrate ESG oversight into board-level governance structures.

3.3. Align ESG Metrics with Financial Systems

- Purpose: Embed ESG data into existing financial reporting processes to create a unified narrative.
- Key Actions:
  - Use enterprise resource planning (ERP) systems to consolidate ESG and financial data.
  - Develop standardized methodologies for calculating and reporting ESG metrics.

3.4. Use Technology for Data Management

- Purpose: Streamline data collection, validation, and analysis to enhance reporting accuracy and efficiency.
- Key Actions:
  - Implement ESG data management platforms to automate reporting processes.
  - Leverage advanced analytics tools to identify trends and generate actionable insights.

3.5. Seek Third-Party Assurance

- Purpose: Enhance the credibility and reliability of ESG disclosures through external validation.
- Key Actions:
  - Engage auditors to verify key ESG metrics and assess alignment with reporting frameworks.
  - Disclose the scope and outcomes of assurance processes in reports.

Section 4: Practical Frameworks and Approaches for ESG Integration

4. Challenges in Implementing Frameworks

Despite their benefits, organizations may encounter challenges when adopting ESG frameworks, including:

4.1. Framework Complexity - Navigating the detailed requirements of frameworks such as TCFD or GRI can be resource-intensive.

- *Solution*: Provide training for finance and sustainability teams to ensure a clear understanding of reporting requirements.

4.2. Overlap Between Frameworks - Multiple frameworks may lead to duplication of efforts or inconsistent reporting.

- *Solution*: Map metrics across frameworks to identify synergies and reduce redundancies.

4.3. Adapting Frameworks to Local Contexts - Global frameworks may not fully address region-specific regulatory or cultural considerations.

- *Solution*: Customize reporting approaches to align with local requirements while adhering to global standards.

5. The Role of finance professionals

Finance professionals are instrumental in implementing ESG frameworks and ensuring their integration with financial reporting. Key responsibilities include:

5.1. Aligning Metrics - Map ESG metrics to financial performance indicators to demonstrate their materiality and relevance.

5.2. Ensuring Data Integrity - Validate ESG data to ensure accuracy, consistency, and alignment with reporting standards.

5.3. Communicating Results - Present integrated ESG and financial reports that resonate with diverse stakeholders, emphasizing transparency and accountability.

Conclusion

Practical frameworks and structured approaches are essential for integrating ESG factors into financial reporting. By adopting leading frameworks such as GRI, SASB, and TCFD, organizations can create robust and credible ESG disclosures that align with stakeholder expectations and regulatory requirements. Finance professionals play a pivotal role in this process, bridging the gap between sustainability and profitability to drive long-term value creation. The next chapter will explore tools and technologies that enable accurate, efficient, and transparent ESG reporting, providing actionable insights for financial and sustainability practitioners.

Tools and Technologies for ESG Reporting

1. Overview of ESG Reporting Tools
2. Advanced Technologies Shaping ESG Reporting
3. Future Trends in ESG Reporting Technology

© 2024 Sekai FM | ESG for finance professionals

Section 1: Overview of ESG Reporting Tools

In the era of digital transformation, tools and technologies play a critical role in enabling accurate, efficient, and transparent ESG reporting. As organizations face increasing demands for comprehensive and credible ESG disclosures, leveraging the right tools is essential to streamline data collection, enhance reporting accuracy, and ensure compliance with global standards. This section provides an overview of key categories of ESG reporting tools, their functionalities, and their impact on improving the quality and reliability of ESG disclosures.

1. The Role of Technology in ESG Reporting

Integrating technology into ESG reporting offers several significant advantages, including:

1.1. Improved Data Accuracy and Consistency

- Automated tools reduce the risk of human error in data collection and processing, ensuring the accuracy of ESG metrics.
- Example: A cloud-based emissions tracking system can automatically calculate carbon footprints based on real-time operational data.

1.2. Streamlined Reporting Processes

- Technology simplifies complex reporting requirements by consolidating data from multiple sources and formats into a unified system.
- Example: ESG platforms can aggregate data from supply chains, operations, and financial systems to produce comprehensive reports.

1.3. Enhanced Transparency and Traceability

- Digital solutions enable organizations to provide granular data, enhancing transparency and trust among stakeholders.
- Example: Blockchain technology can trace supply chain activities, ensuring ethical sourcing and compliance

1.4. Real-Time Monitoring

- Tools that enable real-time data tracking allow organizations to respond proactively to ESG risks and opportunities.
- Example: Monitoring tools can provide alerts for deviations from emissions targets, enabling timely corrective actions.

Section 1: Overview of ESG Reporting Tools

2. Key Categories of ESG Reporting Tools

ESG reporting tools can be broadly categorized based on their functionalities and applications. Understanding these categories helps organizations select the most appropriate tools for their specific needs.

Data Collection and Management Tools

Purpose: Automate the gathering, consolidation, and validation of ESG data from various internal and external sources.

- Integration with enterprise resource planning (ERP) systems to extract operational data.
- Customizable templates for inputting ESG metrics, such as carbon emissions, diversity ratios, or community investment.

Examples:

- Workiva: Provides a platform for collecting and managing ESG data alongside financial reporting.
- Tableau: Offers data visualization capabilities to identify trends and insights in ESG performance.

Analytics and Benchmarking Tools

Purpose: Analyze ESG performance, identify trends, and benchmark metrics against industry standards or peer organizations.

- Predictive analytics to assess potential risks and opportunities.
- Industry-specific benchmarks to evaluate performance relative to competitors.

Examples:

- MSCI ESG Manager: Enables companies to benchmark ESG scores and track progress over time.
- SAS ESG Solutions: Uses advanced analytics to quantify the financial impacts of ESG initiatives.

Reporting and Disclosure Platforms

Purpose: Facilitate the preparation and submission of ESG reports in compliance with global frameworks and regulatory requirements.

- Pre-built templates aligned with standards such as GRI, SASB, and TCFD.
- Automated generation of disclosures tailored to stakeholder-specific needs.

Examples:

- Enablon: Supports multi-framework reporting, ensuring alignment with diverse regulatory and investor requirements.
- EcoVadis: Specializes in ESG disclosure for supply chain reporting and corporate social responsibility (CSR).

Assurance and Verification Tools

Purpose: Enhance the credibility of ESG disclosures by validating data accuracy and compliance with standards.

- Automated audits of ESG metrics to detect anomalies or inconsistencies.
- Integration with third-party assurance providers for independent validation.

Examples:

- Greenstone: Offers tools for tracking and verifying sustainability data.
- ISAE 3000-compliant software: Ensures compliance with international assurance standards for non-financial reporting.

Specialized Tools for ESG Risks

Purpose: Monitor and manage specific ESG risks, such as climate-related risks, ethical supply chain practices, or governance compliance.

- Scenario analysis for climate risks, incorporating variables such as temperature increases or regulatory shifts.
- Supply chain tracking for ethical sourcing and labor compliance.

Examples:

- CarbonChain: Tracks carbon emissions across complex supply chains.
- KPMG Climate IQ: Provides climate risk assessments tailored to financial reporting needs.

Section 1: Overview of ESG Reporting Tools

Conclusion

Tools and technologies are indispensable for modern ESG reporting, offering efficiency, accuracy, and transparency in aligning sustainability performance with financial outcomes. By adopting the right tools, organizations can overcome data challenges, meet stakeholder expectations, and maintain compliance with global standards. In the next section, we will explore advanced technologies and future trends in ESG reporting, highlighting innovations that are shaping the future of sustainable business practices.

Section 2: Advanced Technologies Shaping ESG Reporting

The rapid evolution of technology is revolutionizing ESG reporting, providing organizations with innovative tools to meet growing demands for accuracy, transparency, and efficiency. Advanced technologies, such as artificial intelligence (AI), blockchain, and data analytics, are enabling organizations to overcome traditional challenges in ESG reporting, including data fragmentation, compliance complexities, and stakeholder engagement. This section explores how these technologies are transforming ESG reporting and their implications for finance professionals.

1. Artificial Intelligence (AI) and Machine Learning (ML)

AI and ML are reshaping ESG reporting by automating data collection, analysis, and reporting processes, reducing manual efforts, and improving accuracy.

1.1. Applications in ESG Reporting

- Data Mining and Integration: AI can gather ESG data from diverse sources, such as supplier databases, operational systems, and external reports, creating a unified dataset.
    - Example: AI-powered tools can scan and analyze supplier compliance reports to track labor practices or environmental impacts.
- Predictive Analytics: ML algorithms can forecast ESG risks and opportunities based on historical data and trends.
    - Example: Predictive models can identify areas where emissions targets may not be met, enabling proactive interventions.
- Automated Reporting: AI can generate ESG disclosures aligned with multiple frameworks by automatically mapping data to reporting requirements.

1.2. Benefits

- Accelerates reporting timelines by automating repetitive tasks.
- Enhances data accuracy by reducing human errors in manual data processing.
- Provides actionable insights for decision-making through advanced analytics.

1.3. Challenges

- Requires substantial initial investment and technical expertise.
- May face limitations in processing unstructured data or context-specific metrics.

Section 2: Advanced Technologies Shaping ESG Reporting

2. Blockchain for Transparency and Traceability

Blockchain technology is emerging as a powerful tool for enhancing the transparency and traceability of ESG data, particularly in supply chain reporting and carbon accounting.

2.1. Applications in ESG Reporting

- Supply Chain Transparency: Blockchain creates an immutable ledger of transactions, enabling organizations to verify ethical sourcing and compliance with environmental standards.
    - Example: Companies can track the provenance of raw materials, such as ensuring that minerals are conflict-free.
- Carbon Credit Verification: Blockchain can authenticate carbon credits, reducing the risk of double-counting or fraud in emissions trading schemes.
    - Example: A blockchain-based registry can track the lifecycle of carbon credits from issuance to retirement.

2.2. Benefits

- Increases stakeholder trust by providing tamper-proof records of ESG data.
- Enhances data traceability, particularly in complex supply chains.
- Reduces the administrative burden of audits by offering real-time verification.

2.3. Challenges

- High energy consumption of blockchain networks can contradict sustainability goals.
- Requires collaboration across stakeholders to establish standardized protocols.

Section 2: Advanced Technologies Shaping ESG Reporting

3. Big Data and Advanced Analytics

Big data and advanced analytics enable organizations to process vast volumes of ESG data, uncovering patterns and trends that inform strategic decision-making.

3.1. Applications in ESG Reporting

- Materiality Assessments: Analytics tools can process stakeholder inputs, financial data, and industry benchmarks to identify material ESG issues.
- Performance Monitoring: Real-time dashboards powered by big data enable organizations to track ESG metrics, such as energy usage or employee engagement, across multiple locations.
    - Example: A multinational company can monitor water usage across facilities and identify areas for improvement.
- Scenario Analysis: Advanced analytics can model the financial impacts of ESG risks, such as climate change or regulatory changes, under various scenarios.

3.2. Benefits

- Provides granular insights into ESG performance across operations.
- Enables dynamic reporting by integrating real-time data feeds.
- Improves decision-making by quantifying ESG impacts on financial outcomes.

3.3. Challenges

- Data standardization remains a challenge due to the diverse sources and formats of ESG data.
- Requires investment in robust data infrastructure and analytics expertise.

Section 2: Advanced Technologies Shaping ESG Reporting

4. Internet of Things (IoT) for Real-Time Data Collection

IoT devices are transforming ESG reporting by enabling real-time data collection from physical assets and operational processes.

4.1. Applications in ESG Reporting

- Environmental Monitoring: IoT sensors can measure emissions, water usage, and energy consumption in real time.
  - Example: Sensors installed in factories can monitor air quality and report deviations from regulatory limits.
- Supply Chain Tracking: IoT devices can track the movement and condition of goods, ensuring compliance with environmental and social standards.
  - Example: IoT-enabled trackers can verify that perishable goods are transported under sustainable conditions.

4.2. Benefits

- Reduces the lag in ESG data reporting by providing instant insights.
- Improves accuracy by eliminating manual data collection errors.
- Enables proactive interventions to address ESG risks as they arise.

4.3. Challenges

- High costs of implementing and maintaining IoT infrastructure.
- Security and privacy concerns related to the collection and transmission of sensitive data.

5. Natural Language Processing (NLP) for ESG Insights

NLP, a subset of AI, enables organizations to analyze unstructured data, such as textual ESG reports, social media content, and stakeholder feedback.

5.1. Applications in ESG Reporting

- Sentiment Analysis: NLP tools can analyze stakeholder opinions on ESG issues, providing insights into reputational risks and opportunities.
  - Example: An organization can monitor social media mentions to gauge public sentiment on its sustainability initiatives.
- Regulatory Monitoring: NLP can process and summarize ESG-related regulations, ensuring compliance across jurisdictions.
  - Example: NLP-powered tools can extract relevant clauses from climate policies, streamlining compliance efforts.

5.2. Benefits

- Provides deeper insights into qualitative aspects of ESG performance.
- Enhances stakeholder engagement by identifying emerging concerns.
- Improves efficiency in regulatory compliance and policy analysis.

5.3. Challenges

- May struggle to interpret context-specific or nuanced language.
- Requires highquality training data to ensure accuracy.

Section 2: Advanced Technologies Shaping ESG Reporting

6. Cloud Computing for Scalable ESG Reporting

Cloud computing platforms provide the scalability and flexibility needed to manage large-scale ESG reporting initiatives.

6.1. Applications in ESG Reporting

- Centralized Data Storage: Cloud platforms enable organizations to store and access ESG data from multiple locations in a secure environment.
- Collaborative Reporting: Teams across geographies can collaborate on ESG disclosures in real time using cloud-based tools.

6.2. Benefits

- Reduces IT infrastructure costs by leveraging scalable cloud resources.
- Enhances data accessibility and collaboration, particularly for global organizations.

6.3. Challenges

- Data security and privacy remain critical concerns.
- Dependency on service providers for system reliability and updates.

7. Challenges of Advanced Technologies

Despite their transformative potential, advanced technologies face implementation challenges:

7.1. Integration with Legacy Systems

- Organizations may face difficulties integrating advanced technologies with existing infrastructure.
- Solution: Adopt hybrid systems that bridge legacy platforms with modern tools.

7.2. High Initial Costs

- Advanced technologies often require significant upfront investment in hardware, software, and training.
- Solution: Opt for scalable, subscription-based models to manage costs.

7.3. Skill Gaps

- Effective use of advanced technologies requires specialized skills in AI, blockchain, and data analytics.
- Solution: Invest in capacity-building programs to enhance technical expertise.

Section 2: Advanced Technologies Shaping ESG Reporting

8. The Role of finance professionals

Finance professionals are at the forefront of leveraging advanced technologies to enhance ESG reporting. Their key responsibilities include:

- Technology Adoption: Collaborate with IT teams to identify and implement appropriate ESG tools and technologies.
- Data Analysis: Use advanced analytics to quantify the financial impacts of ESG metrics and communicate findings to stakeholders.
- Stakeholder Engagement: Leverage technology to produce transparent and accessible ESG disclosures tailored to diverse audiences.

Conclusion

Advanced technologies such as AI, blockchain, and IoT are transforming ESG reporting by enhancing data accuracy, transparency, and efficiency. By adopting these innovations, organizations can overcome traditional challenges, meet stakeholder expectations, and align ESG performance with financial outcomes. The next section will explore the future trends in ESG reporting technology, highlighting emerging innovations and their implications for sustainability practices.

Section 3: Future Trends in ESG Reporting Technology

As the demand for comprehensive ESG reporting grows, technological advancements continue to reshape how organizations measure, analyze, and communicate their ESG performance. The future of ESG reporting technology lies in the convergence of emerging innovations such as artificial intelligence (AI), blockchain, the Internet of Things (IoT), and quantum computing. These advancements promise to enhance the precision, transparency, and impact of ESG disclosures, enabling organizations to meet the evolving expectations of regulators, investors, and other stakeholders. This section explores key future trends in ESG reporting technology and their implications for finance professionals.

1. Predictive and Prescriptive Analytics

Predictive and prescriptive analytics will play a transformative role in ESG reporting by moving beyond historical data to forecast future risks and opportunities.

1.1. Predictive Analytics

- Functionality: Uses machine learning algorithms to analyze historical ESG data and predict future trends or risks.
    - Example: Predicting the financial impact of carbon pricing scenarios on an organization's operations.
- Applications:
    - Anticipating regulatory changes and their implications for compliance costs.
    - Identifying trends in stakeholder sentiment related to ESG issues.

1.2. Prescriptive Analytics

- Functionality: Recommends actionable strategies based on predictive insights.
    - Example: Suggesting specific energy efficiency investments to achieve emissions reduction targets.
- Applications:
    - Optimizing resource allocation for sustainability projects.
    - Recommending supply chain adjustments to meet ethical sourcing goals.

Section 3: Future Trends in ESG Reporting Technology

2. Real-Time ESG Reporting

The future of ESG reporting lies in real-time data collection and disclosure, driven by advancements in IoT and cloud-based technologies.

2.1. Real-Time Data Collection

- IoT sensors and devices will enable continuous monitoring of ESG metrics, such as energy consumption, emissions, and water usage.
  - Example: Sensors in manufacturing facilities can provide real-time updates on energy efficiency and emissions levels.

2.2. Instantaneous Reporting

- Cloud platforms and integrated dashboards will allow organizations to generate real-time ESG reports, enhancing transparency and responsiveness.
  - Example: Automatically updating investors on progress toward sustainability goals during earnings calls.

2.3. Implications

- Real-time reporting will enable organizations to address ESG risks proactively, strengthening stakeholder trust and operational resilience.

3. ESG Blockchain Networks

Blockchain will revolutionize ESG reporting by ensuring data integrity, enhancing traceability, and fostering collaboration across supply chains.

3.1. Decentralized Data Verification

- Blockchain's decentralized architecture will provide tamper-proof records of ESG metrics, ensuring the credibility of disclosures.
  - Example: Verifying the authenticity of carbon credits in emissions trading systems.

3.2. Supply Chain Traceability

- Blockchain networks will allow organizations to track and verify sustainability practices across complex supply chains.
  - Example: Ensuring compliance with ethical labor standards for suppliers in multiple countries.

3.3. Collaborative Platforms

- Shared blockchain networks will enable industries to establish common ESG reporting standards and share verified data.
  - Example: A blockchain-based platform for renewable energy providers to share emissions data with stakeholders.

Section 3: Future Trends in ESG Reporting Technology

4. Integration of ESG with Financial Planning and Analysis (FP&A)

ESG will become a fully integrated component of financial planning and analysis, supported by advanced analytics and scenario modeling tools.

4.1. Scenario Modeling

- Organizations will use ESG scenario modeling tools to assess the financial implications of different sustainability strategies.
    - Example: Evaluating the long-term costs and benefits of transitioning to a circular economy model.

4.2. ESG KPIs in Budgeting

- ESG key performance indicators (KPIs) will become central to budgeting and resource allocation processes.
    - Example: Allocating capital based on potential reductions in carbon intensity or improvements in workforce diversity.

4.3. Implications

- Integrating ESG into FP&A will align sustainability goals with financial objectives, enabling organizations to make informed decisions about long-term investments.

5. Quantum Computing for ESG Reporting

Quantum computing, though in its early stages, has the potential to address the computational challenges of large-scale ESG data analysis.

5.1. Advanced Data Analysis

- Quantum computing will process vast ESG datasets at unprecedented speeds, enabling more accurate and complex analyses.
    - *Example*: Modeling global climate change scenarios to assess their financial implications for multinational corporations.

5.2. Optimizing Supply Chains

- Quantum algorithms will optimize supply chain networks to reduce environmental impact and improve efficiency.
    - *Example*: Minimizing transportation emissions while ensuring cost efficiency in logistics.

5.3. Implications

- Quantum computing will unlock new possibilities for ESG reporting, particularly in industries with extensive global operations and complex data requirements.

Section 3: Future Trends in ESG Reporting Technology

6. Enhanced Stakeholder Engagement through AI-Driven Communication

AI-powered tools will transform how organizations engage stakeholders by personalizing ESG communications and enhancing accessibility.

6.1. Natural Language Generation (NLG)

- AI-driven NLG systems will create customized ESG reports tailored to different stakeholder groups, such as investors, employees, or customers.
  - Example: Automatically generating a simplified ESG summary for retail investors and a detailed analysis for institutional investors.

6.2. Interactive Platforms

- AI chatbots and virtual assistants will provide real-time responses to stakeholder queries about ESG performance.
  - Example: An AI assistant on a corporate website answering questions about sustainability initiatives.

6.3. Implications

- These tools will enhance transparency and trust by making ESG data more accessible and engaging for diverse audiences.

7. Integration with Global ESG Ecosystems

Future ESG reporting technologies will seamlessly integrate with global sustainability ecosystems, enabling greater collaboration and standardization.

7.1. Open Data Platforms

- Organizations will contribute to and access open data platforms for ESG reporting, promoting transparency and shared knowledge.
  - Example: Industry-wide platforms where companies can benchmark their ESG performance against peers.

7.2. Unified Frameworks

- Advanced technologies will harmonize reporting across frameworks such as GRI, SASB, and TCFD, reducing duplication and inconsistencies.

7.3. Implications

- Integration with global ecosystems will streamline reporting processes and improve the comparability of ESG disclosures.

Section 3: Future Trends in ESG Reporting Technology

8. Implications for finance professionals

As ESG reporting technologies evolve, finance professionals must adapt to new tools and methodologies to maintain their relevance and effectiveness.

8.1. Enhanced Skillsets

- Professionals will need to develop expertise in emerging technologies such as AI, blockchain, and quantum computing.

8.2. Strategic Decision-Making

- Leveraging predictive analytics and scenario modeling tools will enable finance professionals to align ESG initiatives with long-term business strategy.

8.3. Stakeholder Communication

- Finance professionals will play a central role in interpreting complex ESG data and presenting it in a meaningful way to stakeholders.

Conclusion

The future of ESG reporting lies in the integration of cutting-edge technologies that enhance accuracy, transparency, and stakeholder engagement. From predictive analytics to blockchain networks, these innovations will empower organizations to align sustainability with profitability while meeting the expectations of an increasingly ESG-conscious world. Finance professionals will be at the forefront of this transformation, leveraging these tools to drive strategic value and ensure the credibility of ESG disclosures. The next chapter will discuss practical strategies for communicating ESG performance to stakeholders, focusing on crafting compelling narratives that align with financial and non-financial goals.

Reporting Frameworks and Standards

1. Overview of Major ESG Reporting Frameworks
2. How to Choose the Right ESG Reporting Framework
3. Comparing and Contrasting ESG Reporting Frameworks
4. Best Practices for Implementing ESG Reporting Frameworks

© 2024 Sekai FM | ESG for finance professionals

Section 1: Overview of Major ESG Reporting Frameworks

The growing emphasis on Environmental, Social, and Governance (ESG) issues has led to the development of numerous reporting frameworks and standards that guide organizations in disclosing their ESG performance. These frameworks provide the structure, principles, and metrics necessary to ensure transparency, comparability, and credibility in ESG reporting. However, navigating the multitude of frameworks can be challenging, especially as regulatory requirements evolve and stakeholder expectations diversify. This section provides an overview of the major ESG reporting frameworks, examining their key features, applications, and relevance for finance professionals.

1. The Role of Reporting Frameworks in ESG Disclosure

ESG reporting frameworks serve as blueprints for organizations to systematically collect, measure, and disclose their ESG performance. Their role is critical in:

1.1. Enhancing Transparency and Accountability

- Frameworks ensure organizations disclose material ESG information in a transparent manner, fostering trust among stakeholders.
- Example: Disclosing greenhouse gas (GHG) emissions under a framework such as the GHG Protocol enhances accountability in addressing climate risks.

1.2. Standardizing Disclosures

- By providing consistent methodologies and metrics, frameworks enable comparability across organizations, industries, and geographies.
- Example: Investors can benchmark ESG performance across companies using SASB standards for industry-specific metrics.

1.3. Facilitating Stakeholder Engagement

- Frameworks help organizations identify and communicate material ESG issues that matter most to stakeholders, such as regulators, investors, employees, and customers.

1.4. Supporting Strategic Decision-Making

- ESG disclosures guided by frameworks inform risk assessment, resource allocation, and long-term planning.

Section 1: Overview of Major ESG Reporting Frameworks

2. Overview of Major ESG Reporting Frameworks

The leading ESG reporting frameworks differ in their scope, approach, and target audience. Selecting the right framework depends on the organization's goals, regulatory requirements, and stakeholder priorities.

2.1. Global Reporting Initiative (GRI)

- GRI is one of the most widely used frameworks, focusing on the broader impacts of an organization's activities on the environment, society, and the economy:
  - Emphasizes double materiality, covering financial and non-financial impacts.
  - Offers universal, sector-specific, and topic-specific standards.
- **Strengths**:
  - Suitable for organizations aiming to disclose their sustainability impacts comprehensively.
  - Aligns well with global sustainability initiatives, such as the UN Sustainable Development Goals (SDGs).
- **Relevance to finance professionals:**
  - Provides insights into how ESG factors affect stakeholder relationships and operational risks.

2.2. Sustainability Accounting Standards Board (SASB)

- SASB focuses on financially material ESG issues, offering industry-specific standards for 77 sectors:
  - Designed to meet the needs of investors by linking ESG performance to financial outcomes.
  - Includes metrics tailored to industries such as technology, manufacturing, and financial services.
- **Strengths**:
  - Prioritizes materiality, ensuring disclosures focus on ESG factors that impact financial performance.
  - Facilitates investor decision-making by integrating ESG data into financial analysis.
- **Relevance to finance professionals:**
  - Ideal for aligning ESG disclosures with financial reporting, enabling risk management and investment analysis.

2.3. Task Force on Climate-related Financial Disclosures (TCFD)

- TCFD provides a framework for disclosing climate-related risks and opportunities, emphasizing their financial implications:
  - Organized around four pillars: governance, strategy, risk management, and metrics/targets.
  - Promotes scenario analysis to evaluate potential impacts of climate risks.
- **Strengths**:
  - Helps organizations address investor concerns about climate risks.
  - Encourages integration of climate-related data into financial disclosures.
- **Relevance to finance professionals:**
  - Supports compliance with emerging climate reporting regulations.
  - Enables scenario planning for climate-related financial risks.

2.4. International Integrated Reporting

- <IR> focuses on integrating financial and non-financial data to provide a holistic view of an organization's value creation over time:
  - Highlights six capitals: financial, manufactured, intellectual, human, social, and natural.
  - Encourages organizations to link ESG performance to their overall strategy and business model.
- **Strengths**:
  - Provides a cohesive narrative that connects ESG efforts with financial performance.
  - Promotes long-term value creation and strategic alignment.
- **Relevance to finance professionals:**
  - Bridges the gap between sustainability initiatives and financial strategy.

Section 1: Overview of Major ESG Reporting Frameworks

2. Overview of Major ESG Reporting Frameworks

2.5. Carbon Disclosure Project (CDP)

- CDP specializes in environmental disclosures, focusing on climate change, water security, and deforestation.
- Key Features:
  - Uses a questionnaire-based approach to gather standardized environmental data.
  - Aligns with global frameworks such as TCFD and the Paris Agreement.
- Strengths:
  - Enables organizations to benchmark environmental performance and identify areas for improvement.
  - Well-regarded by investors seeking climate-related data.
- Relevance to finance professionals:
  - Offers detailed insights into environmental risks and opportunities, aiding compliance and strategy development.

3. Choosing the Right Framework

Selecting the appropriate framework depends on several factors:

3.1. Organizational Goals

- Consideration: Is the focus on addressing stakeholder impacts (e.g., GRI) or financial materiality (e.g., SASB)?

3.2. Regulatory Environment

- Consideration: Are there specific reporting requirements, such as TCFD for climate-related disclosures or CSRD for EU companies?

3.3. Industry Context

- Consideration: Does the organization operate in a sector with unique ESG risks, making industry-specific standards (e.g., SASB) more relevant?

3.4. Stakeholder Priorities

- Consideration: What ESG factors are most important to investors, regulators, and other stakeholders?

3.5. Integration with Financial Reporting

- Consideration: How seamlessly can the framework align with existing financial reporting processes and systems?

Section 1: Overview of Major ESG Reporting Frameworks

4. Challenges in Using ESG Frameworks

While frameworks provide essential guidance, their implementation is not without challenges:

4.1. Overlap Between Frameworks

- Organizations often need to comply with multiple frameworks, leading to duplication and complexity.
- Solution: Use technology platforms to map and consolidate overlapping metrics.

4.2. Evolving Standards

- Frequent updates to frameworks require organizations to adapt their reporting processes continuously.
- Solution: Monitor developments in ESG standards and engage with external advisors to stay informed.

4.3. Resource Constraints

- Smaller organizations may lack the resources to adopt comprehensive frameworks.
- Solution: Start with frameworks that prioritize material issues and scale up over time.

5. The Role of finance professionals

Finance professionals play a key role in navigating ESG frameworks by:

- Aligning Metrics: Mapping ESG data to financial outcomes, ensuring disclosures are relevant to investors and regulators.
- Validating Data: Ensuring the accuracy and reliability of ESG metrics reported under selected frameworks.
- Advising Strategy: Guiding organizations in selecting frameworks that align with their goals and stakeholder expectations.
- Communicating Insights: Translating ESG disclosures into actionable insights for decision-makers and stakeholders.

Conclusion

ESG reporting frameworks provide the foundation for transparent, credible, and impactful sustainability disclosures. By understanding the strengths and applications of major frameworks such as GRI, SASB, TCFD, and <IR>, organizations can select the approaches that best meet their strategic and stakeholder needs. For finance professionals, mastering these frameworks is essential to aligning ESG performance with financial reporting and driving long-term value creation. The next section will explore how organizations can choose the most appropriate framework and effectively integrate it into their reporting processes.

© 2024 Sekai FM | ESG for finance professionals

Section 2: How to Choose the Right ESG Reporting Framework

Selecting the right ESG reporting framework is a critical step for organizations aiming to disclose their sustainability performance effectively. Given the plethora of frameworks available, choosing the most suitable one requires a strategic evaluation of organizational goals, stakeholder expectations, regulatory requirements, and industry context. This section provides a detailed guide on how organizations can navigate this complex decision-making process, ensuring that their ESG reporting aligns with both internal objectives and external demands.

1. Understanding the Factors That Influence Framework Selection

The decision to adopt a specific ESG reporting framework should be informed by a combination of strategic, operational, and external considerations.

1.1. Materiality Focus

- Definition: Materiality refers to the ESG issues that are most significant to an organization's financial performance, stakeholders, or societal impact.
- Considerations:
  - Financial Materiality: If the focus is on the financial implications of ESG factors, frameworks such as SASB or TCFD may be most relevant.
  - Double Materiality: For organizations addressing both financial and non-financial impacts, GRI is a preferred choice.
- Example: A technology company might prioritize SASB for industry-specific metrics such as data security, while a manufacturing firm may adopt GRI to disclose broader environmental impacts.

1.2. Regulatory Requirements

- Definition: Regulations increasingly mandate ESG disclosures, often prescribing specific frameworks or standards.
- Considerations:
  - Identify jurisdiction-specific mandates, such as the EU's CSRD, which requires alignment with the European Sustainability Reporting Standards (ESRS).
  - Consider global frameworks that align with regulatory trends, such as TCFD for climate-related disclosures.
- Example: A multinational corporation operating in Europe and the U.S. might adopt both CSRD-aligned ESRS and SASB standards to meet regional compliance and investor expectations.

Section 2: How to Choose the Right ESG Reporting Framework

1. Understanding the Factors That Influence Framework Selection

1.3. Industry Relevance

- Definition: Different industries face unique ESG risks and opportunities, making industry-specific frameworks more relevant.
- Considerations:
    - Evaluate frameworks that provide tailored guidance for the organization's sector.
    - Use SASB for granular industry-focused metrics, or GRI for broader cross-industry applications.
- Example: A financial institution might focus on metrics related to responsible lending and climate risk, while a food and beverage company would emphasize water use and supply chain sustainability.

1.4. Stakeholder Expectations

- Definition: Stakeholders, including investors, customers, employees, and regulators, have varying priorities regarding ESG information.
- Considerations:
    - Investors may prefer SASB or TCFD for financially material disclosures.
    - Customers and employees may value broader impact reporting aligned with GRI or CDP.
- Example: An organization with ESG-focused investors might prioritize TCFD for its financial relevance, while using GRI to engage with consumers and employees on broader sustainability initiatives.

1.5. Integration with Financial Reporting

- Definition: ESG reporting should complement traditional financial disclosures, creating a unified narrative of organizational performance.
- Considerations:
    - Evaluate frameworks like <IR> or SASB for their ability to align ESG metrics with financial reporting.
    - Consider using frameworks that integrate ESG into enterprise risk management systems.
- Example: A company seeking to link sustainability investments to financial outcomes might use <IR> to connect ESG efforts with long-term value creation.

© 2024 Sekar FM | ESG for finance professionals

Section 2: How to Choose the Right ESG Reporting Framework

2. A Step-by-Step Process for Framework Selection

Organizations can use a structured approach to evaluate and select the most appropriate ESG reporting framework.

2.1. Conduct a Materiality Assessment

- Purpose: Identify the ESG issues most relevant to the organization's operations, stakeholders, and regulatory environment:
  - Engage stakeholders through surveys, interviews, and workshops to prioritize ESG topics.
  - Analyze industry benchmarks and peer disclosures to identify common material issues.
- Outcome: A clear understanding of priority ESG issues to guide framework selection.

2.2. Map Reporting Goals to Frameworks

- Purpose: Align the organization's ESG objectives with the focus areas of different frameworks:
  - List reporting goals, such as enhancing investor confidence, complying with regulations, or improving stakeholder engagement.
  - Compare these goals against the scope and strengths of major frameworks.
- Outcome: A shortlist of frameworks that best meet organizational goals.

2.3. Evaluate Resource Availability

- Purpose: Assess the internal capacity and resources required to implement and maintain a reporting framework.
  - Evaluate the availability of ESG data, technology infrastructure, and skilled personnel.
  - Consider frameworks with scalable implementation requirements, such as CDP for focused disclosures or GRI for comprehensive reporting.
- Outcome: A practical choice of framework that aligns with organizational capacity.

2.4. Consider Framework Compatibility

- Purpose: Ensure the chosen framework integrates seamlessly with existing reporting processes and standards:
  - Identify overlaps between financial reporting standards (e.g., IFRS) and ESG frameworks.
  - Use platforms or tools that support multi-framework reporting to streamline disclosures.
- Outcome: A framework that enhances, rather than complicates, existing reporting workflows.

2.5. Pilot the Framework

- Purpose: Test the framework in a limited capacity before full-scale adoption:
  - Implement the framework for a specific ESG metric or business unit.
  - Collect feedback from internal teams and external stakeholders to refine the process.
- Outcome: Confidence in the framework's applicability and effectiveness.

Section 2: How to Choose the Right ESG Reporting Framework

3. Challenges in Framework Selection

Even with a structured approach, organizations may face challenges in selecting the right framework.

3.1. Overlapping Requirements

- Challenge: Many frameworks have overlapping metrics, leading to duplication of efforts.
- Solution: Use integrated reporting tools to consolidate data and streamline reporting across frameworks.

3.2. Evolving Standards

- Challenge: Frameworks are frequently updated to reflect emerging ESG trends, requiring organizations to adapt.
- Solution: Stay informed about changes through professional networks, training, and industry associations.

3.3. Balancing Stakeholder Priorities

- Challenge: Different stakeholder groups may prioritize different frameworks.
- Solution: Adopt a multi-framework approach, leveraging tools to manage the complexity.

4. The Role of finance professionals

finance professionals are essential in guiding the framework selection process, as they bring expertise in aligning ESG disclosures with financial reporting and stakeholder expectations.

4.1. Aligning ESG with Financial Performance

- Map ESG metrics to financial outcomes, ensuring the chosen framework reflects material risks and opportunities.

4.2. Ensuring Compliance

- Identify frameworks that meet current and anticipated regulatory requirements in key markets.

4.3. Communicating with Stakeholders

- Collaborate with sustainability teams to ensure the selected framework addresses diverse stakeholder priorities.

Conclusion

Choosing the right ESG reporting framework is a strategic decision that requires careful evaluation of materiality, regulatory requirements, stakeholder expectations, and organizational capacity. By adopting a structured approach, organizations can select frameworks that not only meet external demands but also align with internal goals for sustainability and long-term value creation. Finance professionals play a critical role in this process, ensuring that ESG reporting integrates seamlessly with financial disclosures and supports effective decision-making. The next section will delve into strategies for comparing and contrasting frameworks to maximize their effectiveness and relevance.

Section 3: Comparing and Contrasting ESG Reporting Frameworks

With the growing importance of ESG disclosures, organizations often face the challenge of navigating multiple reporting frameworks, each with distinct priorities, methodologies, and stakeholder focuses. A clear understanding of how these frameworks compare and contrast is essential for organizations to maximize the value of their ESG reporting efforts. This section critically examines key similarities and differences among leading ESG frameworks, highlighting their unique features and providing guidance for selecting and harmonizing frameworks to meet organizational goals.

1. Key Dimensions for Comparison

When comparing ESG reporting frameworks, organizations should evaluate them based on the following dimensions:

1.1. Scope

- Definition: The breadth of ESG issues covered, ranging from narrowly focused metrics to comprehensive multi-topic coverage.
- Example: GRI encompasses a wide range of ESG topics, while TCFD is focused specifically on climate-related risks and opportunities.

1.2. Materiality

- Definition: The criteria used to determine which ESG issues are material for reporting purposes.
- Example: SASB focuses on financial materiality, targeting ESG factors that directly impact financial performance, whereas GRI considers double materiality, including impacts on society and the environment.

1.3. Target Audience

- Definition: The primary stakeholders for whom the framework is designed.
- Example: TCFD and SASB are investor-focused, while GRI is designed for a broader audience, including regulators, employees, and communities.

1.4. Reporting Approach

- Definition: The methodology and format for disclosures, including metrics, narrative reporting, and qualitative insights.
- Example: SASB emphasizes quantitative, industry-specific metrics, whereas <IR> focuses on narrative disclosures linking ESG and financial performance.

1.5. Alignment with Regulatory and Global Standards

- Definition: The extent to which the framework aligns with emerging regulations and global ESG initiatives.
- Example: CDP is aligned with the Paris Agreement and TCFD, while SASB is increasingly referenced in U.S. regulatory contexts.

Section 3: Comparing and Contrasting ESG Reporting Frameworks

2. Detailed Comparison of Major Frameworks

2.4. International Integrated Reporting Framework (<IR>)

- Scope: Holistic, encompassing financial and non-financial factors influencing long-term value creation.
- Materiality: Focuses on value creation for stakeholders over the short, medium, and long term.
- Target Audience: Investors, boards, and senior management.
- Reporting Approach: Narrative-driven, emphasizing the integration of financial and non-financial disclosures.
- Strengths:
  - Promotes strategic alignment between ESG initiatives and financial goals.
  - Provides a unified framework for integrated reporting.
- Limitations:
  - Limited prescriptive guidance on specific ESG metrics.

2.5. Carbon Disclosure Project (CDP)

- Scope: Specialized, focusing on climate change, water security, and deforestation.
- Materiality: Primarily environmental, with some financial relevance.
- Target Audience: Investors, regulators, and environmental advocates.
- Reporting Approach: Questionnaire-based, with standardized metrics aligned to global climate goals.
- Strengths:
  - Strong alignment with the Paris Agreement and TCFD recommendations.
  - Useful for organizations prioritizing environmental disclosures.
- Limitations:
  - Limited coverage of social and governance factors.

© 2024 Sekar I M | ESG for finance professionals

Section 3: Comparing and Contrasting ESG Reporting Frameworks

3. Harmonizing Multiple Frameworks
Organizations often face the need to adopt multiple frameworks to meet diverse stakeholder and regulatory demands. Harmonizing these frameworks requires a strategic approach.

3.1. Mapping Common Metrics
- Identify overlapping metrics across frameworks, such as emissions disclosures required by GRI, SASB, and TCFD.
- Use technology platforms to consolidate data and streamline reporting processes.

3.2. Aligning Narrative and Quantitative Reporting
- Use frameworks like <IR> to provide a cohesive narrative, supported by quantitative metrics from SASB or GRI.
- Example: Link climate-related financial impacts disclosed under TCFD with broader environmental goals reported under GRI.

3.3. Leveraging Technology
- Adopt ESG reporting software capable of generating reports aligned with multiple frameworks.
- Example: Tools like Enablon or Workiva can map ESG data to multiple reporting standards simultaneously.

3.4. Tailoring Disclosures to Stakeholders
- Customize reports to meet the needs of specific stakeholders, such as using TCFD for investors and GRI for broader audiences.

4. Implications for finance professionals
Finance professionals must navigate the complexities of multiple frameworks, ensuring their alignment with financial reporting and stakeholder expectations.

4.1. Data Integration - Consolidate ESG and financial data to ensure consistency across frameworks.
4.2. Strategic Advisory - Guide organizations in selecting and harmonizing frameworks that align with their goals and compliance requirements.
4.3. Communication - Translate ESG disclosures into actionable insights for stakeholders, emphasizing the connection between sustainability and financial performance.

Conclusion
Comparing and contrasting ESG reporting frameworks highlights the diverse approaches available to organizations, each with its strengths and limitations. By understanding these differences, organizations can select and harmonize frameworks to meet regulatory requirements, stakeholder expectations, and strategic goals. Finance professionals play a pivotal role in this process, ensuring that ESG reporting aligns with financial disclosures and supports long-term value creation. The next chapter will explore best practices for communicating ESG performance effectively, focusing on crafting compelling narratives and engaging stakeholders.

Section 4: Best Practices for Implementing ESG Reporting Frameworks

The successful implementation of ESG reporting frameworks requires a systematic approach that balances compliance, stakeholder expectations, and organizational goals. Best practices ensure that ESG disclosures are accurate, credible, and aligned with global standards, while also fostering transparency and trust among stakeholders. This section outlines the key strategies organizations can adopt to effectively implement ESG reporting frameworks, ensuring their integration into broader business operations and financial reporting processes.

1. Align ESG Reporting with Organizational Strategy
ESG reporting should be closely aligned with the organization's strategic objectives to ensure that disclosures are relevant, actionable, and meaningful.

1.1. Integrate ESG into Business Goals - Incorporate ESG priorities into the organization's mission, vision, and long-term strategy.

- Example: A manufacturing company may align its emissions reduction targets with its overall objective to achieve carbon neutrality by 2035.

1.2. Embed ESG in Governance Structures - Assign clear accountability for ESG reporting within governance frameworks, such as board-level ESG committees.

- Example: A board-level sustainability committee could oversee the implementation of frameworks like TCFD or SASB.

1.3. Link ESG and Financial Metrics - Connect ESG metrics to financial performance indicators, such as cost savings from energy efficiency or revenue growth from sustainable products.

- Example: Reporting on how renewable energy adoption reduces operating costs and mitigates regulatory risks.

2. Develop Robust Data Management Systems
Accurate and reliable ESG data is the foundation of credible reporting. Organizations should establish systems that ensure the quality, consistency, and traceability of ESG data.

2.1. Centralize Data Collection - Use integrated platforms to collect ESG data from various sources, including operational systems, supply chains, and external vendors.

- Example: A cloud-based system that consolidates emissions data, workforce demographics, and governance metrics.

2.2. Standardize Data Validation Processes - Develop protocols for validating ESG data to ensure accuracy and compliance with reporting standards.

- Example: Establish a cross-functional team to review data inputs and outputs before disclosure.

2.3. Leverage Technology - Implement advanced tools, such as AI and IoT, to automate data collection and improve real-time monitoring of ESG performance.

- Example: IoT sensors tracking water usage in real time across multiple facilities.

Section 4: Best Practices for Implementing ESG Reporting Frameworks

3. Select the Right Frameworks for Stakeholder Needs
To maximize the impact of ESG reporting, organizations must select frameworks that align with stakeholder priorities and regulatory requirements.

3.1. Conduct Stakeholder Analysis

- Identify key stakeholders—such as investors, regulators, employees, and customers—and understand their ESG priorities.
  - Example: Investors may prioritize financially material disclosures aligned with SASB, while regulators may require adherence to TCFD or CSRD.

3.2. Balance Multiple Frameworks

- Use a combination of frameworks to address diverse stakeholder needs, harmonizing overlapping requirements to minimize redundancy.
  - Example: Combining GRI for broad sustainability impacts with SASB for financial materiality.

3.3. Align with Regulatory Standards

- Stay updated on regulatory requirements to ensure compliance with mandatory disclosure standards.
  - Example: Aligning EU operations with CSRD and global climate disclosures with TCFD.

4. Build Internal ESG Capacity
A successful ESG reporting program requires skilled professionals who understand both sustainability and financial reporting.

4.1. Train Teams on ESG Frameworks

- Provide training on the methodologies, metrics, and reporting requirements of adopted frameworks.
  - Example: Conduct workshops on SASB's industry-specific metrics or TCFD's scenario analysis.

4.2. Foster Cross-Functional Collaboration

- Establish collaboration between finance, sustainability, risk management, and compliance teams to align ESG and financial reporting.
  - Example: A joint task force ensuring that sustainability data aligns with financial statements.

4.3. Appoint ESG Champions

- Designate leaders or committees to drive ESG initiatives and oversee the implementation of reporting frameworks.
  - Example: An ESG officer responsible for aligning organizational practices with GRI standards.

Section 4: Best Practices for Implementing ESG Reporting Frameworks

5. Ensure Transparency and Credibility

Transparency and credibility are critical for gaining stakeholder trust and ensuring the effectiveness of ESG disclosures.

5.1. Provide Clear and Balanced Reporting

- Disclose both achievements and challenges in ESG performance, offering a realistic view of progress.
    - Example: Reporting on progress toward emissions reduction targets while acknowledging delays in achieving certain milestones.

5.2. Seek Third-Party Assurance

- Engage independent auditors to verify ESG disclosures, enhancing their credibility.
    - Example: Using an assurance provider to validate Scope 1 and Scope 2 emissions data.

5.3. Use Narrative to Complement Data

- Combine quantitative metrics with qualitative narratives to contextualize ESG performance.
    - Example: Explaining how investments in employee wellness programs have improved workforce productivity.

6. Monitor and Adapt to Emerging Trends

ESG reporting is a dynamic field, influenced by evolving regulations, stakeholder expectations, and technological advancements. Organizations must remain agile to stay ahead.

6.1. Track Regulatory Changes

- Monitor updates to global frameworks and regulations, such as new TCFD requirements or CSRD updates.
    - Example: Regularly reviewing updates from the IFRS Foundation on sustainability standards.

6.2. Embrace Innovation

- Explore emerging technologies, such as blockchain for supply chain traceability or AI for predictive ESG analytics.
    - Example: Using blockchain to verify the authenticity of carbon credits in emissions trading.

6.3. Benchmark Against Peers

- Regularly compare ESG performance and reporting practices with industry peers to identify areas for improvement.
    - Example: Benchmarking emissions disclosures against competitors in the same sector.

Section 4: Best Practices for Implementing ESG Reporting Frameworks

7. The Role of finance professionals

Finance professionals are pivotal in implementing ESG reporting frameworks, bringing expertise in data integration, risk management, and strategic communication.

7.1. Align ESG with Financial Strategy

- Integrate ESG disclosures into financial planning, forecasting, and risk management processes.

7.2. Ensure Data Integrity

- Validate ESG data to ensure consistency with financial disclosures, minimizing discrepancies.

7.3. Communicate Value Creation

- Highlight how ESG initiatives contribute to long-term value creation for stakeholders.
    - Example: Demonstrating cost savings from energy efficiency programs in financial terms.

Conclusion

Implementing ESG reporting frameworks is a complex but critical process that requires alignment with organizational strategy, robust data management, stakeholder engagement, and transparency. By adopting best practices, organizations can ensure that their ESG disclosures are credible, impactful, and aligned with global standards. Finance professionals play a vital role in this process, ensuring that ESG reporting integrates seamlessly with financial disclosures and supports sustainable value creation. The next chapter will focus on strategies for effectively communicating ESG performance, emphasizing how to craft compelling narratives that resonate with diverse stakeholders.

10

Communicating ESG Performance

© 2024 Sekai FM | ESG for finance professionals

Section 1: Best Practices for ESG Disclosures

The growing emphasis on Environmental, Social, and Governance (ESG) issues has amplified the importance of clear, transparent, and compelling communication of ESG performance. ESG disclosures are not merely compliance documents; they are strategic tools that shape stakeholder perceptions, influence investment decisions, and drive competitive advantage. To ensure effective communication, organizations must adopt best practices that enhance the clarity, credibility, and relevance of their disclosures. This section explores the principles and strategies that underpin impactful ESG communication, tailored to the needs of diverse stakeholders.

1. Principles of Effective ESG Communication

Effective ESG communication is guided by key principles that ensure disclosures are meaningful and actionable.

1.1. Transparency - Provide complete and honest information about ESG performance, including successes, challenges, and areas for improvement.

- *Example*: Disclosing both progress toward achieving emissions reduction targets and reasons for missing interim milestones.
- Impact: Builds stakeholder trust and enhances the organization's reputation for accountability.

1.2. Materiality - Focus on the ESG issues most relevant to the organization's operations, industry, and stakeholders.

- *Example*: A financial services firm might prioritize disclosures on data security and governance, while a manufacturing company emphasizes environmental impact.
- Impact: Ensures disclosures resonate with stakeholders and highlight areas of strategic importance.

1.3. Consistency - Ensure ESG disclosures are consistent across reporting periods and align with financial reporting.

- *Example*: Aligning ESG metrics with financial data in annual reports to present a cohesive performance narrative.
- Impact: Enhances comparability and credibility, enabling stakeholders to track progress over time.

1.4. Accessibility - Present ESG information in a clear, engaging, and accessible format, tailored to diverse stakeholder needs.

- *Example*: Using visual aids such as charts, graphs, and infographics to simplify complex data.
- Impact: Improves stakeholder understanding and encourages broader engagement.

1.5. Credibility - Substantiate ESG claims with robust data, independent assurance, and alignment with recognized standards.

- *Example*: Verifying emissions data through third-party audits and aligning disclosures with TCFD or GRI standards.
- Impact: Builds confidence among investors, regulators, and other stakeholders.

Section 1: Best Practices for ESG Disclosures

2. Structuring ESG Disclosures

A well-structured ESG disclosure enhances clarity and ensures stakeholders can easily access relevant information.

2.1. Executive Summary - Provide a concise overview of key ESG achievements, challenges, and strategic priorities.

- Example: Highlighting significant milestones, such as achieving carbon neutrality or launching diversity initiatives.

2.2. Materiality Assessment - Outline the process and outcomes of identifying material ESG issues, linking them to business strategy.

- Example: Including a matrix that maps ESG issues by their importance to stakeholders and financial impact.

2.3. Quantitative and Qualitative Metrics - Combine data-driven insights with narratives to provide a balanced view of ESG performance.

- Example: Reporting on emissions reductions alongside case studies of energy efficiency projects.

2.4. Alignment with Standards - Clearly state which reporting frameworks or standards the disclosures align with, such as GRI, SASB, or TCFD.

- Example: Including a table that maps disclosure content to the requirements of specific frameworks.

2.5. Future Outlook - Highlight future ESG goals, initiatives, and strategies, providing stakeholders with a forward-looking perspective.

- Example: Setting specific timelines for achieving net-zero emissions or increasing board diversity.

3. Tailoring ESG Communication to Stakeholders

Different stakeholders have varying priorities and expectations regarding ESG disclosures. Tailoring communication ensures the message resonates effectively.

3.1. Investors

- Focus Areas: Financial materiality, risk management, and long-term value creation.
- Best Practices:
    - Provide detailed disclosures on climate risks, governance practices, and financial impacts of ESG initiatives.
    - Use frameworks like SASB or TCFD to align with investor expectations.

3.2. Regulators

- Focus Areas: Compliance with mandatory ESG reporting standards.
- Best Practices:
    - Ensure disclosures meet regulatory requirements in relevant jurisdictions.
    - Use clear and standardized formats to facilitate regulatory reviews.

Section 1: Best Practices for ESG Disclosures

3. Tailoring ESG Communication to Stakeholders

3.3. Employees

- Focus Areas: Workplace culture, diversity, and alignment with organizational values.
- Best Practices:
  - Highlight initiatives on employee well-being, training, and development.
  - Use internal channels to engage employees with ESG achievements and goals.

3.4. Customers

- Focus Areas: Sustainability of products and services, ethical practices, and brand alignment with values.
- Best Practices:
  - Emphasize responsible sourcing, product sustainability, and community impact.
  - Use marketing campaigns to communicate ESG achievements to customers.

3.5. Communities and NGOs

- Focus Areas: Social and environmental impacts, community engagement, and ethical practices.
- Best Practices:
  - Showcase partnerships and initiatives that benefit local communities or address global challenges.
  - Provide transparent updates on progress and outcomes of ESG programs.

4. Leveraging Technology in ESG Communication

Technology plays a pivotal role in enhancing the accessibility, accuracy, and impact of ESG disclosures.

4.1. Interactive Dashboards

- Use digital dashboards to present real-time ESG performance metrics, allowing stakeholders to explore data interactively.
- Example: A dashboard displaying energy consumption, emissions, and diversity metrics in real time.

4.2. Digital Reports

- Publish ESG reports in digital formats with hyperlinks, videos, and interactive elements to engage stakeholders.
- Example: An interactive online report that includes video testimonials from employees and community partners.

4.3. Social Media and Online Platforms

- Use social media channels to share ESG highlights, engage with stakeholders, and address emerging concerns.
- Example: Posting updates on sustainability milestones and answering stakeholder queries on platforms like LinkedIn and Twitter.

Section 2: Engaging Stakeholders Through ESG Reporting

Engaging stakeholders effectively is a cornerstone of successful ESG reporting. While disclosures provide transparency, meaningful engagement fosters trust, collaboration, and long-term relationships. ESG reporting must go beyond compliance to actively involve stakeholders in the sustainability journey, addressing their concerns, aligning with their priorities, and demonstrating accountability. This section outlines strategies for stakeholder engagement through ESG reporting, emphasizing the importance of dialogue, responsiveness, and tailored communication.

1. Identifying Key Stakeholders

Stakeholder identification is the first step in creating an engagement strategy that aligns with organizational goals and ESG priorities.

1.1. Internal Stakeholders

- Examples: Employees, board members, and leadership teams.
- Engagement Focus:
  - Align ESG initiatives with corporate culture and values.
  - Promote internal accountability and collaboration.
  - **Example**: Regular updates on ESG progress in internal communications or town hall meetings.

1.2. External Stakeholders

Investors, regulators, customers, suppliers, communities, and non-governmental organizations (NGOs).

- Engagement Focus:
  - Investors: Financial materiality and long-term risk mitigation.
  - Regulators: Compliance with ESG reporting standards and laws.
  - Customers: Ethical practices, product sustainability, and transparency.
  - Communities and NGOs: Social and environmental impacts.

1.3. Prioritizing Stakeholders

- Use materiality assessments to determine which stakeholders and issues are most critical to the organization's ESG strategy.
  - **Example**: Mapping stakeholders based on influence and interest, ensuring priority engagement with high-impact groups.

© 2024 Sekar FM | ESG for finance professionals

Section 2: Engaging Stakeholders Through ESG Reporting

2. Tailoring Communication to Stakeholder Needs

Different stakeholders have unique priorities, requiring customized communication strategies to address their specific concerns and interests.

2.1. Investors and Financial Institutions

- Expectations: Data on ESG risks, opportunities, and financial performance.
- Engagement Methods:
  - Provide detailed ESG metrics aligned with SASB, TCFD, or other investor-focused frameworks.
  - Host ESG-focused investor calls and webinars to discuss performance and strategy.
- Example: A company presenting scenario analyses of climate risks during an annual investor meeting.

2.2. Regulators and Policymakers

- Expectations: Compliance with mandatory ESG reporting standards.
- Engagement Methods:
  - Submit reports aligned with regulatory requirements, such as the CSRD or TCFD.
  - Participate in industry consultations to influence and adapt to evolving regulations.
- Example: Proactively disclosing alignment with new climate-related disclosure mandates.

2.3. Employees

- Expectations: Clear alignment between ESG initiatives and workplace values.
- Engagement Methods:
  - Share updates on ESG goals through newsletters, intranet platforms, or employee workshops.
  - Involve employees in sustainability initiatives, such as volunteering or green office programs.
- Example: Hosting a company-wide sustainability day to showcase progress and encourage participation.

2.4. Customers, Communities and NGOs

- Expectations: Ethical sourcing, sustainability in products/services, and alignment with their values. Positive social and environmental impacts, ethical practices, and collaboration.
- Engagement Methods:
  - Highlight ESG achievements in marketing campaigns and product labels.
  - Provide transparent information about supply chain practices and environmental impacts.
  - Partner with NGOs to co-create initiatives addressing local challenges.
  - Hold community forums or listening sessions to gather feedback and foster collaboration.
- Example: A retail company sharing detailed sustainability information on product packaging and online.

Section 2: Engaging Stakeholders Through ESG Reporting

3. Fostering Two-Way Communication
Stakeholder engagement is most effective when it is a dialogue rather than a one-way flow of information.

3.1. Gathering Feedback
- Use surveys, focus groups, and stakeholder consultations to understand stakeholder expectations and concerns.
- Example: Conducting investor surveys to identify ESG metrics most relevant to decision-making.

3.2. Responding to Stakeholder Input
- Demonstrate responsiveness by addressing stakeholder feedback in subsequent ESG disclosures and initiatives.
- Example: Revising supply chain practices to address customer concerns about ethical sourcing.

3.3. Leveraging Digital Channels
- Use social media, webinars, and interactive platforms to facilitate real-time engagement with stakeholders.
- Example: Hosting live Q&A sessions on sustainability topics with senior executives.

4. Building Trust Through Transparency
Transparent communication is essential for building credibility and trust with stakeholders.

4.1. Balanced Reporting
- Acknowledge both successes and challenges, providing a realistic view of ESG performance.
- Example: Reporting on emissions reductions achieved while disclosing barriers to achieving zero-waste operations.

4.2. Third-Party Validation
- Use independent assurance and certifications to validate ESG disclosures.
- Example: Obtaining third-party assurance for greenhouse gas emissions data or ethical labor practices.

4.3. Continuous Updates
- Provide regular updates on ESG progress, ensuring stakeholders remain informed between formal reporting periods.

Example: Quarterly ESG performance updates in investor communications.

© 2024 Sekai FM | ESG for finance professionals

Section 3: Crafting a Compelling ESG Narrative

A compelling ESG narrative is a critical component of effective communication, enabling organizations to connect with stakeholders on a deeper level while presenting their sustainability journey in a transparent and engaging manner. By combining quantitative data with storytelling, organizations can showcase their ESG achievements, demonstrate accountability, and inspire confidence among investors, employees, customers, and communities. This section explores strategies for creating an authentic ESG narrative that resonates with diverse audiences while maintaining credibility.

1. The Role of Storytelling in ESG Communication

Storytelling transforms ESG data into a cohesive narrative that highlights an organization's commitment to sustainability and its broader impact.

1.1. Building Emotional Connections

- Definition: Storytelling humanizes ESG efforts by illustrating how they positively affect individuals, communities, and the planet.
- Example: Sharing stories of employees benefitting from diversity initiatives or communities supported by renewable energy projects.
- Impact: Engages stakeholders emotionally, fostering trust and loyalty.

1.2. Highlighting Purpose

- Definition: A compelling narrative articulates the organization's purpose and its alignment with ESG priorities.
- Example: A company's commitment to innovation and environmental stewardship as part of its broader mission to "drive sustainable progress."
- Impact: Reinforces the organization's long-term vision and values.

1.3. Contextualizing Data

- Definition: Storytelling provides context for ESG metrics, explaining trends, achievements, and challenges.
- Example: Linking a 20% reduction in emissions to specific operational changes, such as transitioning to renewable energy sources.
- Impact: Enhances the relevance and understanding of ESG data.

Section 3: Crafting a Compelling ESG Narrative

2. Key Components of a Strong ESG Narrative

A strong ESG narrative incorporates several elements to ensure clarity, relevance, and authenticity.

2.1. Transparency and Honesty
- Acknowledge challenges alongside achievements to present a balanced and credible story.
    - Example: "While we achieved a 30% reduction in water usage, we are addressing challenges in improving supply chain emissions reporting."

2.2. Alignment with Stakeholder Priorities
- Tailor the narrative to address the concerns and interests of key stakeholder groups.
    - Example: For investors, emphasize how ESG initiatives mitigate risks and drive long-term value creation.

2.3. Demonstration of Impact
- Use data and examples to illustrate the tangible outcomes of ESG initiatives.
    - Example: Highlighting how a renewable energy investment reduced operating costs and carbon emissions.

2.4. Connection to Business Strategy
- Show how ESG initiatives align with the organization's broader strategic goals.
    - Example: Linking sustainable product innovation to growth in new markets and customer satisfaction.

2.5. Future Vision
- Provide a forward-looking perspective on ESG goals and aspirations.
    - Example: Outlining a roadmap to achieve net-zero emissions by 2030.

3. Techniques for Crafting an ESG Narrative

Organizations can use several techniques to create an impactful ESG narrative.

3.1. Use Real Stories
- Share personal stories and testimonials from employees, customers, or communities affected by ESG initiatives. (e.g. eaturing an employee's experience with a workforce diversity program).

3.2. Leverage Visual Storytelling
- Use visuals such as infographics, videos, and photos to make ESG stories more engaging and accessible. (e.g. A video showcasing the installation of solar panels at a manufacturing facility).

3.3. Create a Clear Structure
- Organize the narrative with a beginning, middle, and end to guide the audience through the story. (e.g. Start with the motivation behind an ESG initiative, detail the actions taken, and conclude with the results achieved).

3.4. Use Analogies and Comparisons
- Simplify complex ESG concepts by relating them to familiar ideas or benchmarks. (e.g. Describing emissions reductions as equivalent to taking 50,000 cars off the road).

© 2024 Sekar EM | ESG for finance professionals

Section 3: Crafting a Compelling ESG Narrative

4. Channels for Delivering the ESG Narrative

The choice of communication channels influences how effectively the ESG narrative reaches and engages stakeholders.

4.1. Annual and Sustainability Reports
- Usage: Comprehensive documents combining data, analysis, and stories to showcase ESG performance.
- Best Practices: Use infographics and case studies to make reports more engaging.

4.2. Digital Platforms
- Usage: Websites, social media, and online dashboards offer real-time and interactive ways to share the ESG narrative.
- Best Practices: Create dedicated ESG web pages and use social media for updates and stakeholder interaction.

4.3. Media and Public Relations
- Usage: Leverage press releases, interviews, and media campaigns to amplify key ESG messages.
- Best Practices: Partner with credible media outlets to enhance reach and credibility.

4.4. Direct Stakeholder Engagement
- Usage: Town halls, webinars, and meetings provide opportunities for direct communication and dialogue.
- Best Practices: Use these forums to gather feedback and strengthen relationships with stakeholders.

5. Avoiding Common Pitfalls in ESG Storytelling

Organizations must be cautious to ensure their ESG narrative remains credible and impactful.

5.1. Greenwashing: Overstating or misrepresenting ESG achievements.
- Solution: Focus on verified data, seek third-party assurance, and be transparent about limitations.

5.2. Lack of Specificity: Using vague or generic statements that lack substance.
- Solution: Provide concrete examples and metrics to back up claims.

5.3. Ignoring Challenges: Omitting difficulties or setbacks, leading to skepticism.
- Solution: Acknowledge challenges and outline steps to address them.

5.4. Overcomplicating the Message: Using technical jargon or excessive detail that alienates non-expert audiences.
- Solution: Use simple, clear language and visuals to make the narrative accessible.

Section 3: Crafting a Compelling ESG Narrative

6. The Role of finance professionals

Finance professionals are instrumental in shaping the ESG narrative by ensuring accuracy, alignment, and strategic relevance.

6.1. Data Validation

- Ensure all metrics used in the narrative are accurate, consistent, and aligned with reporting standards.

6.2. Strategic Framing

- Highlight the financial implications of ESG initiatives, such as cost savings or risk mitigation.

6.3. Stakeholder Collaboration

- Work with sustainability and communications teams to tailor the narrative to different stakeholder needs.

Conclusion

Crafting a compelling ESG narrative is an essential element of effective ESG communication. By combining data, storytelling, and transparency, organizations can demonstrate their commitment to sustainability while engaging stakeholders and building trust. Finance professionals play a key role in this process, ensuring that the narrative is accurate, strategic, and aligned with organizational goals. The next section will focus on creating impactful ESG disclosures tailored to specific stakeholder groups, emphasizing strategies for maximizing relevance and engagement.

Section 4: Tailoring ESG Disclosures for Specific Stakeholders

Tailoring ESG disclosures to meet the diverse needs and expectations of stakeholders is critical to effective communication. Each stakeholder group—investors, regulators, employees, customers, communities, and NGOs—has distinct priorities, requiring customized disclosures that resonate with their interests. This section explores strategies for tailoring ESG reports and communications to different audiences, ensuring that the message is relevant, impactful, and actionable.

1. Understanding Stakeholder Priorities

Effective ESG disclosures start with a deep understanding of stakeholder expectations and how they align with the organization's ESG strategy.

1.1. Investors

- Priorities: Financial materiality, risk management, and long-term value creation.
- Key Interests:
  - Climate risks and opportunities (e.g., aligned with TCFD).
  - Governance practices and board accountability.
  - Financial impacts of ESG initiatives.

1.2. Regulators

- Priorities: Compliance with ESG reporting standards and alignment with legal requirements.
- Key Interests:
  - Accuracy and completeness of disclosures.
  - Alignment with frameworks such as CSRD, GRI, or TCFD.
  - Evidence of progress on regulatory commitments, such as carbon neutrality.

1.3. Employees

- Priorities: Workplace culture, diversity and inclusion, and alignment with personal values.
- Key Interests:
  - Employee well-being programs.
  - Training and development opportunities.
  - Organizational commitment to ethical and sustainable practices.

1.4. Customers

- Priorities: Product sustainability, ethical sourcing, and alignment with values.
- Key Interests:
  - Transparency about supply chain practices.
  - Environmental impact of products or services.
  - Alignment of the brand with sustainability goals.

1.5. Communities and NGOs

- Priorities: Social impact, environmental stewardship, and collaboration.
- Key Interests:
  - Initiatives benefiting local communities.
  - Efforts to mitigate negative environmental impacts.
  - Collaboration with NGOs on shared goals.

Section 4: Tailoring ESG Disclosures for Specific Stakeholders

2. Strategies for Tailoring ESG Disclosures

Tailoring ESG disclosures involves adapting the format, content, and communication channels to suit the intended audience. Best practices include:

2.1. Investors:

- Focus on financially material metrics, such as emissions intensity, workforce productivity, and governance risk.
- Use frameworks like SASB or TCFD to align disclosures with investor expectations.
- Provide scenario analyses to highlight the financial implications of climate risks.
- Example: A financial report detailing the projected impact of carbon pricing on operational costs.

2.2. Regulators:

- Ensure accuracy and completeness of mandatory disclosures.
- Align with global standards such as GRI or regional requirements like CSRD.
- Provide clear documentation of methodologies and data validation processes.
- Example: A compliance report demonstrating adherence to new environmental regulations.

2.3. Employees:

- Use internal communications channels, such as newsletters or town halls, to share ESG updates.
- Highlight programs and policies that directly impact employees, such as diversity initiatives or mental health programs.
- Solicit employee feedback to align ESG efforts with workforce priorities.
- Example: A newsletter celebrating progress toward gender equity in leadership roles.

2.4. Customers:

- Use marketing materials and product labeling to communicate sustainability attributes.
- Share stories and data about ethical sourcing and environmental impact reductions.
- Engage customers through social media and interactive campaigns.
- Example: A product label highlighting "100% recycled materials" and a QR code linking to the company's sustainability report.

2.5. Communities and NGOs:

- Publish reports that focus on social and environmental impact, using accessible language.
- Highlight partnerships and initiatives that address local challenges.
- Involve communities in shaping and implementing ESG initiatives.
- Example: A community-focused report detailing the organization's contributions to local education and healthcare projects.

Section 4: Tailoring ESG Disclosures for Specific Stakeholders

3. Using Appropriate Channels for Stakeholder Engagement

The choice of communication channels determines how effectively tailored disclosures reach stakeholders.

3.1. Digital Platforms

- Application:
  - Interactive dashboards for real-time ESG data sharing with investors and regulators.
  - Social media campaigns to reach customers and the general public.
- Example: A corporate sustainability microsite offering customizable ESG performance data.

3.2. Reports and Publications

- Application:
  - Detailed sustainability reports for regulators and investors.
  - Summarized brochures or fact sheets for employees and customers.
- Example: A visually engaging annual ESG report highlighting key metrics and stories.

3.3. Direct Engagement

- Application:
  - Webinars and meetings for investors and analysts.
  - Community forums for local engagement.
- Example: Hosting a webinar to discuss the organization's climate strategy with institutional investors.

4. Measuring the Effectiveness of Tailored Disclosures

Organizations must evaluate the impact of their ESG disclosures to ensure they meet stakeholder expectations.

4.1. Feedback Mechanisms

- Use surveys, focus groups, and stakeholder consultations to gather insights on disclosure effectiveness.
- Example: Conducting post-disclosure surveys with investors to assess the clarity and relevance of ESG data.

4.2. Engagement Metrics

- Track engagement levels, such as the number of report downloads, webinar participants, or social media interactions.
- Example: Monitoring how many customers scanned a QR code on product packaging to access sustainability information.

4.3. Benchmarking

- Compare disclosure practices against industry peers to identify areas for improvement.
- Example: Analyzing how competitors communicate Scope 3 emissions data.

Section 4: Tailoring ESG Disclosures for Specific Stakeholders

5. The Role of finance professionals

Finance professionals are instrumental in tailoring ESG disclosures to diverse stakeholder needs.

5.1. Data Integration

- Ensure that ESG data aligns with financial reporting to enhance credibility and relevance.

5.2. Stakeholder Analysis

- Collaborate with sustainability and communications teams to identify and address the priorities of each stakeholder group.

5.3. Impact Assessment

- Use financial expertise to assess and articulate the economic implications of ESG initiatives.

Conclusion

Tailoring ESG disclosures to the needs of specific stakeholder groups is essential for maximizing the impact of ESG communication. By aligning content, format, and channels with stakeholder priorities, organizations can foster trust, enhance engagement, and demonstrate their commitment to sustainability. Finance professionals play a key role in this process, ensuring that disclosures are accurate, relevant, and strategically aligned. The next section will focus on overcoming challenges in ESG communication, exploring solutions to common obstacles and strategies for maintaining credibility and consistency.

Section 5: Overcoming Challenges in ESG Communication

As organizations strive to meet increasing demands for transparent and impactful ESG disclosures, they often encounter challenges that can undermine the effectiveness of their communication strategies. These obstacles range from inconsistent data and evolving regulatory requirements to skepticism and accusations of greenwashing. Overcoming these challenges is essential for maintaining credibility, building trust, and aligning ESG reporting with strategic goals. This section explores common challenges in ESG communication and offers solutions to address them effectively.

1. Common Challenges in ESG Communication

1.1. Inconsistent or Incomplete Data

- Problem: ESG data often originates from multiple sources, leading to inconsistencies, inaccuracies, or gaps in reporting.
- Impact: Undermines the credibility of disclosures and complicates stakeholder comparisons.
- Example: Variability in supply chain emissions data due to differing measurement standards across suppliers.

1.2. Evolving Regulatory Landscape

- Problem: Rapidly changing ESG reporting regulations and standards create challenges for compliance and consistency.
- Impact: Organizations may struggle to meet regulatory expectations and adapt reporting processes.
- Example: The introduction of the EU's Corporate Sustainability Reporting Directive (CSRD) requiring double materiality reporting.

1.3. Skepticism and Accusations of Greenwashing

- Problem: Stakeholders may perceive ESG disclosures as exaggerated or misleading, especially if claims are unsupported by evidence.
- Impact: Erodes stakeholder trust and exposes organizations to reputational risks.
- Example: Criticism of companies promoting carbon neutrality while investing in carbon-intensive activities.

1.4. Balancing Complexity and Clarity

- Problem: ESG reporting often involves technical jargon and complex metrics, making it difficult for non-expert stakeholders to understand.
- Impact: Reduces stakeholder engagement and limits the accessibility of disclosures.
- Example: Overloading reports with excessive technical data without clear narratives or visual aids.

1.5. Lack of Integration with Financial Reporting

- Problem: Disjointed ESG and financial disclosures fail to provide a holistic view of organizational performance.
- Impact: Weakens the strategic value of ESG reporting for investors and decision-makers.
- Example: Separate ESG and annual financial reports with no alignment of metrics or narratives.

Section 5: Overcoming Challenges in ESG Communication

2. Solutions for Overcoming ESG Communication Challenges

2.1. Establish Robust Data Management Processes - Invest in systems and protocols that ensure the consistency, accuracy, and completeness of ESG data.

- Key Actions:
  - Use technology platforms to centralize data collection and validation.
  - Standardize data reporting across departments and supply chains.
- *Example*: Implementing a software solution that automates data integration from operational systems to ESG reporting frameworks.

2.2. Stay Ahead of Regulatory Changes - Monitor evolving regulations and align ESG reporting with global and regional standards.

- Key Actions:
  - Engage with industry groups and regulatory bodies to stay informed.
  - Use frameworks such as GRI, SASB, and TCFD as a foundation for compliance.
- *Example*: Preparing for CSRD requirements by aligning existing disclosures with the European Sustainability Reporting Standards (ESRS).

2.3. Ensure Transparency to Address Skepticism - Be honest about both achievements and challenges, and support all claims with verified data.

- Key Actions:
  - Seek third-party assurance for critical metrics such as carbon emissions or diversity ratios.
  - Acknowledge areas for improvement and outline plans to address them.
- *Example*: Publishing an independent auditor's report alongside ESG disclosures to validate accuracy.

2.4. Simplify Communication for Accessibility

- Solution: Present ESG data in a clear, concise, and engaging manner that resonates with diverse audiences.
- Key Actions:
  - Use infographics, charts, and visuals to simplify complex data.
  - Provide executive summaries with key insights for non-expert stakeholders.
- *Example*: A sustainability report featuring a one-page summary of key ESG achievements and visualized metrics.

2.5. Integrate ESG and Financial Reporting

- Solution: Create unified reports that align ESG performance with financial metrics and strategic objectives.
- Key Actions:
  - Use frameworks like the International Integrated Reporting Framework (<IR>) to connect ESG and financial disclosures.
  - Highlight how ESG initiatives contribute to financial outcomes, such as cost savings or risk mitigation.
- *Example*: Including a section in the annual financial report that details the financial impacts of sustainability projects.

© 2024 Sekar FM | ESG for finance professionals

Section 5: Overcoming Challenges in ESG Communication

3. Leveraging Technology to Address Challenges

Advanced technology solutions can help organizations overcome communication challenges by improving data accuracy, enhancing transparency, and streamlining reporting.

3.1. Data Management Platforms

- Use platforms like Workiva, Enablon, or Tableau to centralize ESG data collection and reporting.

3.2. Predictive Analytics

- Leverage AI and machine learning to forecast ESG risks and opportunities, providing actionable insights for stakeholders.

3.3. Blockchain for Transparency

- Use blockchain to verify supply chain data and ensure the integrity of ESG disclosures.

3.4. Interactive Dashboards

- Provide real-time updates on ESG performance through interactive dashboards tailored to different stakeholders.

4. Measuring Success in ESG Communication

To ensure effectiveness, organizations must evaluate the impact of their ESG communication strategies.

4.1. Stakeholder Feedback

- Use surveys, focus groups, and consultations to gather feedback on ESG disclosures.
- Example: An investor survey assessing the clarity and relevance of climate risk disclosures.

4.2. Engagement Metrics

- Track indicators such as report downloads, social media interactions, and webinar attendance.
- Example: Monitoring the number of views and shares of a sustainability video on LinkedIn.

4.3. Benchmarking

- Compare ESG communication practices against industry peers to identify strengths and areas for improvement.
- Example: Analyzing how competitors disclose Scope 3 emissions to enhance reporting practices.

Section 5: Overcoming Challenges in ESG Communication

5. The Role of finance professionals

Finance professionals are essential in addressing ESG communication challenges by ensuring the accuracy, consistency, and relevance of disclosures.

5.1. Data Oversight

- Validate ESG data to align it with financial reporting standards.

5.2. Strategic Alignment

- Ensure ESG initiatives and metrics are integrated into the organization's strategic goals.

5.3. Stakeholder Communication

- Translate technical ESG data into actionable insights for investors, regulators, and other stakeholders.

Conclusion

Overcoming challenges in ESG communication is critical for ensuring transparency, building trust, and driving meaningful stakeholder engagement. By adopting robust data management practices, staying ahead of regulatory changes, and simplifying complex information, organizations can create credible and impactful ESG disclosures. Finance professionals play a vital role in this process, ensuring that ESG communication aligns with organizational goals and supports long-term value creation. The next chapter will focus on assurance and verification in ESG reporting, exploring methods to validate disclosures and enhance their credibility.

Assurance and Verification in ESG Reporting

1. The Importance of Assurance in ESG Reporting
2. Methods and Approaches for Effective ESG Verification
3. Working with External Auditors

© 2024 Sekai FM | ESG for finance professionals

Section 1: The Importance of Assurance in ESG Reporting

As Environmental, Social, and Governance (ESG) reporting gains prominence, stakeholders demand greater accuracy, transparency, and accountability in disclosures. Assurance, the independent verification of ESG data and processes, has emerged as a critical tool to enhance the credibility of ESG reports. This section examines the importance of assurance in ESG reporting, its role in building stakeholder trust, and the challenges organizations face in implementing robust assurance processes.

1. The Need for Assurance in ESG Reporting

1.1. Growing Scrutiny of ESG Disclosures

- Investors, regulators, and customers are increasingly scrutinizing ESG claims to ensure alignment with regulatory requirements and ethical standards.
- Misstatements or inaccuracies can lead to reputational damage, regulatory penalties, and loss of stakeholder trust.
- Example: Companies overstating their environmental performance or underreporting climate risks risk accusations of greenwashing.

1.2. Ensuring Data Accuracy and Reliability

- ESG data often comes from diverse sources and involves complex metrics, increasing the risk of errors or inconsistencies.
- Independent assurance validates the accuracy and reliability of ESG metrics, providing confidence in the data's integrity.
- Example: Assurance verifies key metrics such as carbon emissions, water usage, and workforce diversity, ensuring they meet global standards.

1.3. Meeting Regulatory and Investor Expectations

- Regulatory bodies and investors increasingly mandate assurance for ESG disclosures, aligning them with financial audit standards.
- Example: The European Union's Corporate Sustainability Reporting Directive (CSRD) requires third-party assurance for sustainability reports.

2. Benefits of Assurance in ESG Reporting

Assurance provides significant benefits to organizations, stakeholders, and the broader ESG ecosystem.

2.1. Enhancing Credibility and Trust

- Assurance builds confidence among stakeholders that ESG disclosures are accurate, complete, and aligned with recognized standards.
- Example: Verified claims about renewable energy use or ethical sourcing practices reassure investors and customers.

2.2. Strengthening Stakeholder Relationships

- Transparent and assured ESG reporting fosters stronger relationships with stakeholders, who value accountability and authenticity.
- Example: Assurance helps engage ESG-focused investors by demonstrating the organization's commitment to responsible practices.

© 2024 Sekai FM | ESG for finance professionals

Section 1: The Importance of Assurance in ESG Reporting

2. Benefits of Assurance in ESG Reporting

2.3. Supporting Decision-Making

- Assurance provides management with reliable data, enabling informed decision-making on sustainability initiatives.
- Example: Verified emissions data supports strategic investments in energy efficiency or carbon offset programs.

2.4. Mitigating Risks

- Assurance identifies potential gaps or inaccuracies in ESG reporting, reducing the risk of reputational damage or regulatory non-compliance.
- Example: An assurance provider identifies gaps in a company's Scope 3 emissions reporting, enabling corrective action.

2.5. Aligning with Global Standards

- Assurance ensures that ESG disclosures align with frameworks such as GRI, SASB, or TCFD, enhancing comparability and compliance.
- Example: A TCFD-aligned assurance process ensures climate-related disclosures meet investor expectations.

3. The Role of Assurance Providers

Independent assurance providers, including auditing firms, certification bodies, and consultants, play a central role in verifying ESG data and processes.

3.1. Scope of Assurance

- Assurance providers assess a range of ESG metrics, including:
  - Environmental metrics: Carbon emissions, water usage, energy efficiency.
  - Social metrics: Diversity and inclusion, labor practices, community engagement.
  - Governance metrics: Board composition, ethical practices, compliance with regulations.

3.2. Types of Assurance

- Limited Assurance: Provides a moderate level of confidence in ESG disclosures, often focusing on specific metrics.
  - Example: Verifying Scope 1 and Scope 2 emissions data.
- Reasonable Assurance: Provides a higher level of confidence, involving more detailed testing and analysis.
  - Example: Verifying comprehensive sustainability performance across multiple ESG dimensions.

3.3. Methodologies

- Assurance providers follow internationally recognized standards, such as:
  - ISAE 3000: International standard for assurance engagements on non-financial data.
  - AA1000AS: Assurance standard focusing on inclusivity, materiality, and responsiveness in sustainability reporting.

Section 1: The Importance of Assurance in ESG Reporting

4. Challenges in Implementing ESG Assurance

While assurance is essential, organizations face challenges in adopting robust assurance processes.

4.1. Data Complexity - ESG data often comes from disparate systems, making it difficult to ensure consistency and accuracy.

- Solution: Implement centralized data management systems to streamline data collection and validation.

4.2. Lack of Standardization - The absence of universally accepted ESG reporting standards complicates assurance processes.

- Solution: Align disclosures with leading frameworks such as GRI, SASB, or TCFD to facilitate assurance.

4.3. Costs of Assurance - Assurance engagements can be costly, particularly for organizations with extensive ESG disclosures.

- Solution: Prioritize assurance for high-impact or high-risk metrics to maximize value.

4.4. Expertise Gaps - Assurance requires expertise in both ESG principles and technical methodologies, which may be lacking in some organizations.

- Solution: Collaborate with experienced assurance providers and invest in internal capacity building.

5. The Future of Assurance in ESG Reporting

The role of assurance in ESG reporting will continue to grow as stakeholders demand higher standards of transparency and accountability.

5.1. Integration with Financial Audits

- ESG assurance will increasingly align with financial audits, creating a unified approach to corporate reporting.
- Example: Auditors assessing both financial performance and ESG metrics in integrated reports.

5.2. Technology-Enabled Assurance

- Advanced technologies such as AI and blockchain will streamline assurance processes, enhancing data verification and traceability.
- Example: Blockchain ensuring real-time validation of supply chain sustainability metrics.

5.3. Regulatory Mandates

- Governments and regulators will continue to expand requirements for third-party assurance of ESG disclosures. (e.g. Mandatory assurance for biodiversity and social impact metrics under evolving EU regulations).

5.4. Harmonization of Standards

- The development of global ESG assurance standards will simplify processes and improve comparability across organizations. (e.g. The ISSB establishing uniform assurance guidelines).

Section 1: The Importance of Assurance in ESG Reporting

Conclusion

Assurance is a vital component of ESG reporting, enhancing the credibility, transparency, and impact of sustainability disclosures. By verifying ESG data and processes, assurance builds stakeholder trust, supports strategic decision-making, and ensures compliance with global standards. As the ESG landscape continues to evolve, organizations must prioritize robust assurance processes to meet growing stakeholder demands and maintain their competitive edge. The next section will explore methodologies and approaches for effective ESG verification, providing practical insights for organizations and assurance providers.

Section 2: Methods and Approaches for Effective ESG Verification

ESG verification is a rigorous process designed to ensure that an organization's ESG disclosures are accurate, consistent, and aligned with global standards. The methods and approaches used for verification depend on the scope of ESG metrics, the complexity of data, and the frameworks adopted. This section provides an in-depth exploration of key verification methodologies, highlighting best practices for organizations seeking to strengthen the credibility of their ESG reports.

1. Key Methods of ESG Verification

Organizations can choose from various methods to verify their ESG data, each suited to specific metrics and reporting requirements.

1.1. Internal Verification - The organization conducts its own internal review of ESG data before external publication. Approach:

  - Establish cross-functional ESG review teams comprising finance, sustainability, and compliance experts.
  - Use internal controls and audits to verify the accuracy of ESG metrics.
- Strengths:
  - Cost-effective and ensures alignment with internal processes.
  - Improves data ownership within the organization.
- Limitations:
  - Lacks the independence of third-party assurance, which can limit credibility.

1.2. External Assurance - Independent third parties, such as audit firms or certification bodies, verify ESG disclosures. Approach:

  - Engage professional assurance providers with expertise in ESG reporting frameworks (e.g., GRI, SASB, TCFD).
  - Follow international standards like ISAE 3000 or AA1000AS.
- Strengths:
  - Enhances stakeholder confidence through independent validation.
  - Mitigates risks associated with data inaccuracies or greenwashing allegations.
- Limitations:
  - Higher cost compared to internal verification processes.

1.3. Certification Program - Organizations obtain certifications for specific ESG metrics or practices.

  - Participate in programs like Science-Based Targets initiative (SBTi) for emissions or B Corporation certification for social and environmental performance.
- Strengths:
  - Demonstrates compliance with recognized standards.
  - Provides a competitive advantage in stakeholder perception.
- Limitations:
  - Certification processes can be time-consuming and require substantial documentation.

Section 2: Methods and Approaches for Effective ESG Verification

2. Approaches to ESG Verification

2.1. Materiality-Focused Verification

- Definition: Prioritize verification of ESG metrics most relevant to the organization's stakeholders and financial performance.
- Implementation:
  - Conduct materiality assessments to identify high-impact metrics.
  - Allocate resources to verify metrics such as emissions, diversity ratios, or supply chain practices.
- Example: A financial institution verifying climate risk disclosures in alignment with TCFD recommendations.

2.2. Framework-Specific Verification

- Definition: Tailor verification processes to the requirements of specific ESG frameworks.
- Implementation:
  - Use GRI or SASB standards as a basis for assurance engagements.
  - Ensure metrics align with framework-specific definitions and methodologies.
- Example: A manufacturer verifying Scope 3 emissions in compliance with GHG Protocol standards.

2.3. Continuous Monitoring and Verification

- Definition: Implement systems for real-time data monitoring and periodic verification of ESG metrics.
- Implementation:
  - Use IoT devices and data analytics tools for continuous data tracking.
  - Schedule periodic audits to validate the accuracy of reported metrics.
- Example: An energy company monitoring emissions data in real time and conducting quarterly reviews.

2.4. Stakeholder-Driven Verification

- Definition: Involve stakeholders in the verification process to ensure disclosures address their concerns.
- Implementation:
  - Conduct stakeholder consultations during verification to identify areas of interest.
  - Share assurance reports with stakeholders for feedback.
- Example: A consumer goods company engaging NGOs to verify ethical sourcing claims.

Section 2: Methods and Approaches for Effective ESG Verification

Best Practices for Effective ESG Verification

3.1. Establish Robust Governance Structures

- Action: Assign accountability for ESG verification to senior leadership or dedicated committees.
- Example: An ESG committee overseeing data validation processes and assurance engagements.

3.2. Leverage Technology

- Action: Use advanced tools like AI, blockchain, and analytics platforms to streamline verification processes.
- Example: Blockchain enabling transparent tracking of supply chain data to verify ethical sourcing practices.

3.3. Collaborate with Experienced Providers

- Action: Partner with assurance providers or consultants with deep expertise in ESG reporting frameworks.
- Example: Engaging a global auditing firm to verify TCFD-aligned climate risk disclosures.

3.4. Integrate ESG and Financial Reporting Verification

- Action: Align ESG verification processes with financial audits to create a unified assurance approach.
- Example: A combined audit of financial performance and carbon reduction initiatives.

3.5. Focus on Transparency

- Action: Publish assurance reports detailing the scope, methodologies, and findings of verification engagements.
- Example: Including assurance statements in sustainability reports to enhance stakeholder trust.

4. Challenges in ESG Verification

4.1. Data Fragmentation

- Challenge: ESG data is often fragmented across departments and systems, complicating verification.
- Solution: Implement centralized data management platforms to consolidate and standardize metrics.

4.2. Lack of Standardized Metrics

- Challenge: Inconsistent definitions and methodologies across frameworks create barriers to verification.
- Solution: Use widely recognized standards such as GRI or SASB to guide metric definitions.

4.3. High Costs

- Challenge: Comprehensive verification can be resource-intensive, especially for large organizations.
- Solution: Focus on material metrics and high-impact areas to optimize assurance budget.

Section 3: Working with External Auditors

External auditors play a vital role in enhancing the credibility and reliability of ESG reporting. By providing independent assurance, they help organizations validate their sustainability data, comply with regulatory requirements, and build trust with stakeholders. This section explores the process of collaborating with external auditors, from selecting the right assurance partner to preparing for the assurance engagement and leveraging audit outcomes.

1. The Role of External Auditors in ESG Reporting

External auditors bring expertise, independence, and objectivity to the ESG assurance process.

1.1. Independent Validation - External auditors provide unbiased assessments of ESG disclosures, ensuring that data aligns with accepted frameworks and methodologies.

- Example: Auditors verifying carbon emissions data for alignment with the GHG Protocol.

1.2. Enhancing Credibility - Independent assurance from reputable firms increases stakeholder confidence in ESG disclosures.

- Example: A sustainability report validated by a Big Four audit firm reassures investors of data accuracy.

1.3. Ensuring Regulatory Compliance - External auditors help organizations meet regulatory requirements by aligning disclosures with evolving standards.

- Example: Assisting companies in meeting the EU's CSRD assurance mandates.

2. Selecting the Right External Auditor

Choosing the right assurance provider is critical for ensuring a successful ESG audit.

2.1. Evaluate Expertise in ESG Frameworks - Ensure the auditor has experience with the relevant ESG standards (e.g., GRI, SASB, TCFD).

- Example: Selecting an auditor with proven expertise in verifying climate-related financial disclosures.

2.2. Assess Industry Knowledge - Choose auditors familiar with the organization's industry to ensure context-specific insights.

- Example: A manufacturing company selecting an auditor with expertise in environmental metrics like energy efficiency and waste management.

2.3. Verify Credentials and Independence - Ensure the auditor is accredited by recognized bodies and operates independently to avoid conflicts of interest.

- Example: Engaging an ISO 14065-certified firm to audit greenhouse gas (GHG) inventories.

2.4. Consider Scalability and Global Reach - For multinational organizations, select an auditor with a global footprint to streamline assurance across jurisdictions.

- Example: A global corporation engaging an international audit firm to align its disclosures across multiple regions.

Section 3: Working with External Auditors

3. Preparing for an ESG Assurance Engagement

Thorough preparation is essential for a smooth and effective assurance process.

3.1. Define the Scope of Assurance

- Identify the metrics, frameworks, and reporting boundaries to be covered in the audit.
- *Example*: Deciding whether to audit Scope 1 and Scope 2 emissions or include Scope 3 as well.

3.2. Gather and Organize Data

- Consolidate ESG data from various systems, ensuring consistency and completeness.
- *Example*: Using a centralized ESG platform to collect data on energy consumption, water use, and social impact metrics.

3.3. Align Internal Processes with Audit Requirements

- Conduct an internal review to identify and address potential data gaps or inconsistencies.
- *Example*: Performing a pre-assurance gap analysis to ensure readiness for the external audit.

3.4. Engage Stakeholders

- Involve key stakeholders, including sustainability teams, finance departments, and senior management, to support the assurance process.
- *Example*: A cross-functional task force working with auditors to address data verification challenges.

4. Conducting the Assurance Engagement

The assurance engagement involves a detailed review of ESG disclosures, methodologies, and supporting evidence.

4.1. Initial Planning

- The auditor conducts a preliminary assessment to understand the organization's reporting processes and risks.
- *Example*: Identifying material ESG metrics and high-risk areas, such as supply chain emissions.

4.2. Testing and Verification

- The auditor verifies ESG data through sampling, site visits, and review of supporting documentation.
- *Example*: Visiting production facilities to validate energy efficiency data.

4.3. Reporting Findings

- The auditor provides an assurance statement summarizing their findings and the level of assurance achieved (e.g., limited or reasonable).
- *Example*: An assurance statement confirming that water usage data aligns with GRI standards.

© 2024 Selan F M | ESG for finance professionals

Section 3: Working with External Auditors

5. Leveraging Audit Outcomes

The results of the assurance process can inform future ESG strategies and reporting improvements.

5.1. Addressing Audit Recommendations

- Implement corrective actions to address gaps or weaknesses identified during the audit.
- Example: Strengthening data collection processes for Scope 3 emissions based on audit feedback.

5.2. Enhancing Stakeholder Communication

- Use the assurance statement to reinforce the credibility of ESG disclosures in stakeholder communications.
- Example: Including the auditor's findings in annual ESG reports and investor presentations.

5.3. Continuous Improvement

- Integrate audit insights into ongoing ESG reporting and strategy development.
- Example: Updating data management systems to align with audit recommendations for improved accuracy.

6. Challenges in Working with External Auditors

While external assurance adds value, organizations may face challenges in the process.

6.1. High Costs

- External audits can be resource-intensive, particularly for comprehensive ESG reports.
- Solution: Focus on high-priority metrics and high-risk areas to optimize costs.

6.2. Data Accessibility

- Organizations may struggle to provide auditors with complete and consistent data.
- Solution: Invest in centralized data management systems to streamline access and validation.

6.3. Evolving Standards

- Constant updates to ESG frameworks can complicate the assurance process.
- Solution: Stay informed of regulatory changes and align disclosures with globally recognized standards.

Section 3: Working with External Auditors

The Role of finance professionals in External Audits

Finance professionals play a critical role in collaborating with external auditors to ensure a successful ESG assurance engagement.

7.1. Supporting Data Accuracy

- Validate ESG metrics to align them with financial reporting standards and external assurance requirements.

7.2. Facilitating Communication

- Serve as a liaison between the audit team and internal stakeholders to address queries and provide documentation.

7.3. Implementing Recommendations

- Integrate audit findings into financial and operational processes to enhance future reporting.

Conclusion

Working with external auditors is an essential step in building trust, ensuring compliance, and enhancing the credibility of ESG reporting. By selecting experienced assurance providers, preparing thoroughly for the engagement, and leveraging audit outcomes, organizations can demonstrate accountability and align their sustainability efforts with stakeholder expectations. Finance professionals play a pivotal role in facilitating the assurance process and integrating its insights into corporate strategies. The next chapter will conclude the book with a future outlook on ESG, exploring emerging trends and the evolving role of finance professionals in driving sustainable business practices.

Conclusion and Future Outlook

© 2024 Sekai FM | ESG for finance professionals

Section 1: The Evolving Role of ESG in Business

Environmental, Social, and Governance (ESG) factors have transformed from peripheral concerns to central elements of corporate strategy and performance. As stakeholders increasingly prioritize sustainability and ethical governance, the role of ESG in business continues to evolve, shaping operational decisions, financial outcomes, and reputational capital. This section explores the driving forces behind the growing importance of ESG, its integration into business models, and the implications for organizations aiming to remain competitive and responsible in a dynamic global environment.

1. The Shifting Paradigm of ESG in Business

The rise of ESG as a critical business consideration reflects broader societal, regulatory, and market trends that demand greater accountability and sustainability from organizations.

1.1. Stakeholder Expectations

- Investors demand robust ESG disclosures to assess long-term risks and opportunities.
- Customers increasingly favor brands that align with their values on sustainability and social impact.
- Employees expect organizations to champion diversity, inclusion, and ethical practices.

- Impact:
    - Organizations must demonstrate a clear commitment to ESG principles to attract and retain stakeholders.
    - Example: Companies with strong ESG reputations, such as Patagonia and Unilever, have built loyal customer bases and motivated workforces.

1.2. Regulatory Pressures

- Governments and regulatory bodies are introducing stringent ESG disclosure requirements, such as the EU's Corporate Sustainability Reporting Directive (CSRD).
- International agreements, such as the Paris Climate Accord, drive corporate accountability for environmental impact.

- Impact:
    - Compliance with evolving regulations is essential to avoid penalties and maintain market access.
    - Example: Financial institutions face increasing scrutiny on how they account for climate risks in their portfolios under TCFD guidelines.

1.3. Financial Materiality

- ESG factors increasingly influence financial performance, from operational costs to investment attractiveness.
- Climate risks, supply chain disruptions, and governance failures directly affect shareholder value.

- Impact:
    - Organizations that proactively manage ESG risks and opportunities gain a competitive advantage in attracting capital and mitigating financial volatility.
    - Example: Companies with high ESG scores often enjoy lower borrowing costs and higher investor confidence.

© 2024 Sekar J M | ESG for finance professionals

Section 1: The Evolving Role of ESG in Business

2. Integration of ESG into Core Business Functions

The successful integration of ESG into business models requires embedding sustainability and governance considerations into decision-making at all levels.

2.1. Strategic Alignment

- Organizations are aligning ESG initiatives with their broader business strategies to ensure long-term value creation.
- Examples:
  - Incorporating renewable energy investments into operational planning to reduce carbon footprints.
  - Developing ESG-linked executive compensation plans to drive accountability.

2.2. Innovation and Product Development

- ESG considerations are driving innovation in product design and service delivery, ensuring alignment with sustainability goals.
- Examples:
  - Developing energy-efficient technologies in the automotive industry.
  - Creating sustainable packaging solutions in consumer goods.

2.3. Risk Management

- ESG factors are now integral to enterprise risk management, with a focus on identifying and mitigating sustainability and governance risks.
- Examples:
  - Assessing climate risks in real estate portfolios.
  - Monitoring supply chains for compliance with labor and environmental standards.

3. Implications of ESG for the Global Business Landscape

The increasing importance of ESG is reshaping industries, creating new opportunities, and posing challenges for organizations.

3.1. Opportunities

- Market Differentiation: Companies with strong ESG practices can differentiate themselves in crowded markets.
- Access to Capital: ESG-aligned businesses are more attractive to investors seeking sustainable portfolios.
- Resilience and Adaptability: ESG initiatives improve organizational resilience to environmental and social shocks.

3.2. Challenges

- Data Complexity: Measuring and reporting ESG performance remains a challenge, particularly for multinational organizations.
- Regulatory Compliance: Keeping pace with evolving ESG regulations across jurisdictions requires significant resources.
- Stakeholder Alignment: Balancing the diverse priorities of stakeholders can complicate ESG strategy development.

Section 1: The Evolving Role of ESG in Business

4. The Future of ESG in Business

The role of ESG in business will continue to expand, driven by advancements in technology, evolving stakeholder priorities, and global sustainability challenges.

4.1. Technology as an Enabler
- Innovations in AI, IoT, and blockchain will enhance ESG data collection, analysis, and transparency.
- Example: Blockchain technology enabling real-time tracking of supply chain sustainability metrics.

4.2. Emerging Frameworks and Standards
- The harmonization of ESG reporting standards will simplify compliance and improve comparability.
- Example: The International Sustainability Standards Board (ISSB) aims to create unified global ESG reporting standards.

4.3. Broadening ESG Scope
- ESG considerations will expand to include emerging issues such as biodiversity loss, water scarcity, and social justice.
- Example: Investors increasingly evaluate corporate impacts on natural capital and community equity.

4.4. Collaboration and Partnership
- Cross-sector collaborations will become essential to addressing global ESG challenges.
- Example: Public-private partnerships to develop infrastructure for renewable energy and sustainable urban development.

5. The Role of finance professionals in the Evolving ESG Landscape

Finance professionals will play an increasingly pivotal role in integrating ESG into corporate strategy and reporting.

5.1. Driving ESG Integration
- Financial teams must align ESG initiatives with financial goals and reporting processes.
- Example: Quantifying the financial benefits of sustainability projects, such as cost savings from energy efficiency.

5.2. Ensuring Data Accuracy and Credibility
- Finance professionals are key to validating ESG data and ensuring compliance with global standards.
- Example: Implementing robust assurance processes for carbon emissions data.

5.3. Engaging Stakeholders
- Finance teams must communicate the value of ESG initiatives to investors, regulators, and other stakeholders.
- Example: Highlighting how ESG investments mitigate risks and enhance shareholder value.

Section 1: The Evolving Role of ESG in Business

Conclusion

The evolving role of ESG in business reflects a paradigm shift toward sustainability and accountability as drivers of long-term value creation. Organizations that integrate ESG into their strategies and operations are better positioned to navigate emerging risks, capitalize on opportunities, and meet stakeholder expectations. Finance professionals, with their expertise in data analysis, risk management, and strategic communication, are central to this transformation. The next section will explore future trends and emerging issues in ESG, providing insights into how organizations can prepare for the challenges and opportunities that lie ahead.

Section 2: Future Trends and Emerging Issues in ESG

As ESG continues to evolve, organizations must prepare for new challenges and opportunities driven by shifting stakeholder expectations, advancing technologies, and global sustainability goals. The future of ESG reporting will be characterized by greater integration, standardization, and innovation, requiring organizations to stay agile and forward-thinking. This section explores the emerging trends and issues shaping the ESG landscape, offering insights into how businesses can remain competitive and impactful in the years ahead.

1. Greater Integration of ESG and Financial Reporting
The convergence of ESG and financial reporting will define the next phase of corporate disclosure practices, aligning sustainability performance with financial outcomes.

1.1. ESG as a Core Element of Financial Strategy - ESG metrics will increasingly be treated as financial material factors, influencing valuation, risk assessment, and investment decisions.e.g Climate risks integrated into financial models to forecast impacts on asset values or operating costs.

1.2. Unified Reporting Standard - The development of global reporting standards by bodies like the International Sustainability Standards Board (ISSB) will drive the integration of ESG and financial disclosures. e.g. Organizations aligning with ISSB standards to ensure consistency and comparability across jurisdictions.

1.3. ESG in Financial Audits - Auditors will expand their scope to include assurance of ESG metrics alongside traditional financial audits. e.g Auditing firms providing combined reports that verify financial performance and sustainability outcomes.

2. Increasing Regulatory and Market Pressures
The regulatory landscape for ESG reporting is becoming more complex and demanding, requiring organizations to stay ahead of compliance requirements.

2.1. Expanding Regulatory Mandates - Governments and regulatory bodies are implementing stricter ESG disclosure requirements, particularly on climate risks, biodiversity, and social issues. e.g. The European Union's CSRD and the SEC's proposed climate-related disclosure rules.

2.2. ESG in Capital Markets - Investors and financial institutions are embedding ESG criteria into investment and lending decisions, incentivizing organizations to prioritize ESG performance. e.g. Banks integrating climate risk metrics into credit assessments for corporate borrowers.

2.3. Accountability for Supply Chain Practices - Regulatory frameworks will increasingly require organizations to monitor and disclose ESG performance across their supply chains.e.g. The German Supply Chain Due Diligence Act, which mandates reporting on human rights and environmental practices in global supply chains.

Section 2: Future Trends and Emerging Issues in ESG

3. Adoption of Advanced Technologies

Technological innovation will play a crucial role in enhancing ESG reporting, enabling organizations to collect, analyze, and disclose data more effectively.

3.1. Real-Time Data Tracking

- Internet of Things (IoT) sensors and smart technologies will facilitate real-time monitoring of environmental metrics such as emissions, energy consumption, and water usage.
- Example: Factories using IoT to monitor air quality and immediately report deviations from environmental standards.

3.2. Artificial Intelligence (AI) for Predictive Analytics

- AI will enhance ESG risk modeling and predictive analytics, helping organizations anticipate and mitigate sustainability risks.
- Example: AI-driven tools identifying potential supply chain disruptions caused by climate events.

3.3. Blockchain for Transparency

- Blockchain technology will improve traceability and accountability, particularly in supply chain reporting and carbon credit validation.
- Example: Using blockchain to verify ethical sourcing of raw materials, such as conflict-free minerals.

4. Expansion of ESG Scope

The ESG agenda will broaden to address emerging issues and risks, requiring organizations to adapt their strategies and disclosures.

4.1. Biodiversity and Natural Capital

- Biodiversity loss and natural capital preservation will gain prominence as critical environmental issues alongside climate change.
- Example: Disclosing impacts on ecosystems and dependencies on natural resources in alignment with frameworks like the Taskforce on Nature-related Financial Disclosures (TNFD).

4.2. Water Scarcity and Resource Management

- Water use and conservation will become central to ESG reporting, particularly in industries with high water dependencies.
- Example: Reporting water use efficiency metrics in water-intensive sectors like agriculture and manufacturing.

4.3. Social Justice and Equity

- Issues such as income inequality, racial justice, and community impact will receive greater attention in social reporting.
- Example: Companies setting measurable goals for closing pay gaps and improving workforce diversity.

Section 2: Future Trends and Emerging Issues in ESG

5. Heightened Focus on Stakeholder Engagement

Organizations will place greater emphasis on actively engaging stakeholders to align ESG strategies with their expectations.

5.1. Co-Creation of ESG Initiatives

- Stakeholders will increasingly participate in shaping ESG goals and programs.
- Example: Collaborating with community leaders to design and implement local environmental projects.

5.2. Transparent Communication

- Organizations will adopt more interactive and accessible ESG communication methods, leveraging digital platforms to share progress and gather feedback.
- Example: Interactive dashboards allowing stakeholders to explore real-time ESG data.

5.3. Addressing Stakeholder-Specific Concerns

- Tailoring ESG disclosures to specific stakeholder groups will remain a priority.
- Example: Investors prioritizing financial materiality metrics while employees focus on workplace diversity and inclusion.

6. Challenges in the Evolving ESG Landscape

While these trends offer opportunities, they also present challenges that organizations must address to succeed in the future ESG landscape.

6.1. Balancing Complexity and Clarity

- With expanding ESG requirements and metrics, organizations will face difficulties in simplifying complex data for diverse audiences.
- Solution: Adopt structured reporting frameworks and use technology to create clear and concise disclosures.

6.2. Addressing Data Gaps

- Emerging issues like biodiversity and Scope 3 emissions require data that many organizations are not yet equipped to collect.
- Solution: Invest in robust data collection systems and partnerships to enhance reporting capabilities.

6.3. Avoiding Greenwashing

- The growing scrutiny of ESG claims increases the risk of reputational damage from unverified or exaggerated disclosures.
- Solution: Prioritize independent assurance and transparent communication of limitations.

© 2024 Sekar FM | ESG for finance professionals

Section 2: Future Trends and Emerging Issues in ESG

7. Implications for finance professionals

Finance professionals will continue to play a pivotal role in shaping the future of ESG reporting and strategy.

7.1. Integration of ESG and Financial Performance

Finance teams will align ESG initiatives with financial reporting to demonstrate the tangible value of sustainability investments.
***Example**: Highlighting cost savings from energy efficiency projects or revenue growth from sustainable products.*

7.2. Enhancing ESG Data Accuracy

Finance professionals will ensure the integrity of ESG data by adopting robust internal controls and collaborating with external assurance providers.
***Example**: Validating Scope 1 and Scope 2 emissions data for regulatory and investor disclosures.*

7.3. Engaging Stakeholders Through Reporting

Finance teams will craft clear & actionable disclosures to communicate ESG performance effectively to investors, regulators, & other stakeholders.
***Example**: Publishing integrated reports that align financial results with ESG outcomes.*

Conclusion

The future of ESG is marked by both opportunities and challenges as organizations navigate evolving expectations, emerging risks, and transformative technologies. By staying proactive, leveraging innovation, and expanding their scope of impact, businesses can position themselves as leaders in sustainability and accountability. Finance professionals will remain integral to this journey, driving the alignment of ESG with financial performance and ensuring the credibility of disclosures. The final section will provide actionable recommendations for organizations and finance professionals to prepare for and thrive in the evolving ESG landscape.

Section 3: Recommendations for Organizations and Financial Professionals

To thrive in the rapidly evolving ESG landscape, organizations and finance professionals must adopt proactive strategies that align sustainability with long-term value creation. This final section provides actionable recommendations for enhancing ESG reporting, strengthening stakeholder trust, and positioning businesses for success in a sustainability-driven economy.

1. Recommendations for Organizations

1.1. Develop a Comprehensive ESG Strategy

- Action: Establish a clear ESG vision and integrate it into the organization's core business strategy.
  - Conduct materiality assessments to identify key ESG priorities:
  - Set measurable goals and align them with global standards such as the UN SDGs.
  - Regularly review and update the strategy to address emerging risks and opportunities.
- Example: A company committing to achieve net-zero emissions by 2040 and embedding this goal into operational plans and investment decisions.

1.2. Strengthen Data Management Capabilities

- Action: Build robust systems for collecting, managing, and analyzing ESG data to ensure accuracy and transparency:
  - Invest in centralized ESG data platforms to streamline reporting processes.
  - Train employees to understand and adhere to ESG data standards.
  - Use technology such as IoT, AI, and blockchain to enhance data quality and traceability.
- Example: A retailer implementing blockchain to track and report the sustainability of its supply chain.

1.3. Enhance Stakeholder Engagement

- Action: Foster meaningful dialogue with stakeholders to align ESG initiatives with their expectations:
  - Tailor ESG communications to different stakeholder groups, such as investors, employees, and communities.
  - Use interactive platforms like webinars and dashboards for real-time updates and feedback.
  - Involve stakeholders in co-creating ESG initiatives.
- Example: Partnering with local communities to design projects that mitigate environmental impact while creating jobs.

1.4. Prioritize Assurance and Credibility

- Action: Strengthen the credibility of ESG disclosures through independent assurance and transparent reporting:
  - Engage reputable third-party auditors to verify key ESG metrics.
  - Publish detailed assurance statements in sustainability reports.
  - Be transparent about limitations and challenges in ESG performance.
- Example: A manufacturing firm publishing a third-party assurance report on its carbon neutrality claims.

Section 3: Recommendations for Organizations and Financial Professionals

2. Recommendations for finance professionals

2.1. Align ESG and Financial Reporting

- Action: Integrate ESG metrics into financial reports to demonstrate the impact of sustainability on business performance:
  - Use frameworks like <IR> to connect ESG initiatives with financial outcomes.
  - Highlight the financial implications of ESG risks and opportunities, such as cost savings from renewable energy or regulatory fines avoided.
  - Collaborate with sustainability teams to ensure consistent messaging.
- Example: Including energy cost savings from solar installations as part of a company's annual financial disclosures.

2.2. Build Expertise in ESG Frameworks

- Action: Develop deep knowledge of ESG reporting standards and assurance methodologies to guide organizational efforts:
  - Take courses or certifications in frameworks like GRI, SASB, and TCFD.
  - Stay updated on changes to ESG standards and best practices.
  - Serve as an internal advisor on ESG reporting and assurance.
- Example: A CFO completing a TCFD training program to guide the organization's climate risk disclosures.

2.3. Lead on Data Accuracy and Assurance

- Action: Ensure the reliability and credibility of ESG data through rigorous oversight and collaboration with assurance providers:
  - Establish internal controls to validate ESG data before external reporting.
  - Work closely with external auditors during assurance engagements.
  - Address audit findings promptly to improve future disclosures.
- Example: A financial team implementing robust validation processes for Scope 3 emissions data.

2.4. Foster Stakeholder Confidence

- Action: Use clear and transparent communication to build trust with investors, regulators, and other stakeholders:
  - Translate complex ESG metrics into meaningful insights for stakeholder groups.
  - Publish integrated reports that align ESG and financial performance narratives.
  - Host regular ESG-focused investor calls to discuss progress and challenges.
- Example: An organization hosting a webinar to explain its strategy for achieving net-zero emissions and answering investor questions.

2.5. Embrace Continuous Learning and Adaptation

- Action: Stay informed about emerging ESG trends, technologies, and risks to maintain relevance and competitiveness:
  - Attend ESG conferences and participate in industry working groups.
  - Explore innovative tools and methodologies, such as predictive analytics and blockchain.
  - Share learnings and best practices within the organization.
- Example: A financial leader piloting AI-driven tools to forecast the financial impacts of climate change on supply chain costs.

Section 3: Recommendations for Organizations and Financial Professionals

3. Creating a Roadmap for Future ESG Success

Organizations and finance professionals can create a roadmap for ESG success by focusing on long-term sustainability and stakeholder alignment.

3.1. Set Ambitious but Achievable Goals

- Establish bold ESG targets aligned with global benchmarks while ensuring they are realistic and measurable.

3.2. Embrace Innovation

- Leverage emerging technologies to enhance data collection, reporting, and stakeholder engagement.

3.3. Collaborate Across Sectors

- Partner with industry peers, governments, and NGOs to drive collective impact on pressing ESG challenges.

3.4. Monitor Progress

- Use KPIs and regular reviews to track performance, identify gaps, and refine strategies over time.

3.5. Communicate Impact

- Share progress and results in a way that resonates with stakeholders, building trust and reinforcing the organization's commitment to sustainability.

Conclusion

The path forward in ESG reporting requires organizations and finance professionals to act with foresight, agility, and purpose. By aligning sustainability initiatives with financial performance, leveraging technology, and maintaining transparency, businesses can navigate the complexities of the evolving ESG landscape while creating value for stakeholders. Finance professionals will continue to be at the forefront of this transformation, ensuring that ESG efforts are credible, impactful, and integrated into long-term strategies. The journey toward a sustainable future is a collective one, and with proactive measures, organizations can lead the way in addressing global challenges and opportunities.

© 2024 Sekai FM | ESG for finance professionals

Appendix

© 2024 Sekai FM | ESG for finance professionals

The appendices provide additional resources and tools to enhance the understanding and implementation of ESG reporting. These materials are designed to complement the main content of the book, offering practical guidance, definitions, templates, and references for further learning.

Appendix A: Glossary of ESG Terms

This glossary defines key terms and concepts related to ESG reporting, ensuring clarity and consistency for readers.

Key Terms

- Carbon Footprint: The total greenhouse gas emissions caused directly or indirectly by an individual, organization, or product.

- Circular Economy: An economic model aimed at minimizing waste and maximizing resource efficiency by reusing, repairing, and recycling materials.

- Double Materiality: The concept that ESG reporting should consider both financial materiality (impact on the organization) and environmental/social materiality (impact of the organization).

- Greenwashing: Misleading stakeholders about the environmental benefits or sustainability of a product, service, or organization.

- Scope 1, 2, and 3 Emissions: Categories of greenhouse gas emissions defined by the GHG Protocol:
    - Scope 1: Direct emissions from owned or controlled sources.
    - Scope 2: Indirect emissions from purchased energy.
    - Scope 3: All other indirect emissions in the value chain.

- Task Force on Climate-related Financial Disclosures (TCFD): A framework for climate-related financial risk disclosures.

- Sustainability Accounting Standards Board (SASB): A standard-setting body providing industry-specific ESG reporting guidance.

© 2024 Sekar FM | ESG for finance professionals

Appendix B: Additional Resources

B.1: Key Organizations and Standards

Global Reporting Initiative (GRI): www.globalreporting.org

Sustainability Accounting Standards Board (SASB): www.sasb.org

Task Force on Climate-related Financial Disclosures (TCFD): www.fsb-tcfd.org

Carbon Disclosure Project (CDP): www.cdp.net

International Integrated Reporting Council (<IR>): www.integratedreporting.org

B.2: Recommended Reading

- Sustainability Reporting: Concepts, Frameworks, and Global Practices by GRI.
- Climate Risk and Financial Performance: Insights from TCFD.
- Integrated Thinking: Building Better Organizations by IIRC.

B.3: Online Tools and Platforms

- ESG Data Platforms: Enablon, Workiva, Diligent.
- Climate Risk Analytics: SBTi Target Validation Tool, Carbon Tracker.
- Community Engagement Tools: Benevity, Fluxx.

Appendix C: Frequently Asked Questions (FAQs)

C.1: What is ESG Reporting?

ESG reporting involves disclosing a company's environmental, social, and governance practices and performance to stakeholders.

C.2: Why is ESG Important for finance professionals?

Finance professionals are key to integrating ESG into financial strategies, ensuring transparency, and aligning ESG initiatives with long-term value creation.

C.3: What Are the Benefits of ESG Reporting?

- Enhanced investor confidence.
- Improved risk management.
- Stronger stakeholder relationships.
- Alignment with regulatory requirements.

C.4: How Do I Choose an ESG Framework?

Select a framework based on your industry, stakeholder priorities, and the type of materiality most relevant to your organization (e.g., financial vs. double materiality).

www.ingramcontent.com/pod-product-compliance
Lightning Source LLC
LaVergne TN
LVHW082334200926
848481LV00012B/3349